RULES

OF

RESILIENCE

RULES OF RESILIENCE

10 Ways Successful People Get Better, Wiser, and Stronger

VALORIE BURTON

TYNDALE
REFRESH®
Think Well. Live Well. Be Well.

Visit Tyndale online at tyndale.com.

Tyndale, Tyndale's quill logo, *Tyndale Refresh*, and the Tyndale Refresh logo are registered trademarks of Tyndale House Ministries. Tyndale Refresh is a nonfiction imprint of Tyndale House Publishers, Carol Stream, Illinois.

MAXWELL LEADERSHIP and the Maxwell Leadership logo are trademarks of The John Maxwell Company, LLC, and are used herein by permission of The John Maxwell Company, LLC.

Rules of Resilience: 10 Ways Successful People Get Better, Wiser, and Stronger

Cover design by Lindsey Bergsma

Interior design and scale illustration by Laura Cruise

Published in association with The Bindery Agency, www.TheBinderyAgency.com.

For information about special discounts for bulk purchases, please contact Tyndale House Publishers at csresponse@tyndale.com, or call 1-855-277-9400.

Library of Congress Cataloging-in-Publication Data

A catalog record for this book is available from the Library of Congress.

ISBN 979-8-4005-0525-6

Printed in the United States of America

31 30 29 28 27 26 25
7 6 5 4 3 2 1

I dedicate this book to my son, Alex,
who is a blessing of resilience.

You are loved.
You are kind.
You are smart.
You have God's wisdom inside of you when
you just remember to ask for it.
And you can do hard things!

I love you,
Mom

CONTENTS

FOREWORD

Resilience is a word we truly understand only when life demands it from us. The storms of life are inevitable—setbacks, losses, changes we didn't anticipate. But resilience isn't about avoiding those storms. It's about having the strength, the tools, and the mindset to navigate them and come out stronger on the other side.

The most successful people aren't those who avoid challenges; they're the ones who face them head-on, learn from them, and adapt. They take the lessons from hardship and use them to climb higher. That's why I'm thrilled about *Rules of Resilience*. Valorie Burton has given us a manual for thriving in a world filled with uncertainty and change.

Let me tell you something about Valorie: She's not just an expert in resilience; she embodies it. Her approach to helping people rise above life's challenges is rooted in wisdom, experience, and a deep understanding of what it means to grow through adversity. She doesn't simply teach resilience; she equips you to practice it in real, practical ways.

I remember a story Valorie once shared with me about a young entrepreneur she coached. This person had faced setback after setback—failed launches, financial strain, and mounting self-doubt. But through Valorie's guidance, she realized that resilience wasn't about pretending everything was fine or pushing through blindly. It was about creating a system: learning to manage her energy, focusing on what she could control, and reframing setbacks as opportunities to grow. With time, this businesswoman not only recovered but built a thriving business grounded in lessons learned from those difficult moments.

That's the power of resilience—it transforms not just how you face challenges but how you grow because of them. And in *Rules of Resilience*, Valorie lays out the steps to enable you to do just that. This isn't a book of theories; it's a tool kit filled with practical strategies, insightful stories, and actionable advice. Valorie guides you to build the kind of resilience that doesn't just help you bounce back—it helps you move forward.

What I love most about this book is its clarity. Valorie doesn't overwhelm you with lofty ideas. She offers simple, straightforward rules that you can apply to your life immediately. Whether you're navigating a personal challenge, leading a team, or looking to strengthen your mindset, these principles will meet you where you are and help you move toward where you want to be.

As you read this book, I encourage you to let it challenge and stretch you. Reflect on Valorie's coaching questions, put her practices into action, and give yourself the grace to grow. Resilience is not a trait you're born with—it's a skill you build. And the work is worth it because the stronger your resilience, the greater your impact on the world around you.

So dive in. Let these pages encourage you, strengthen you, and equip you. With *Rules of Resilience* as your guide, you'll discover not only the power of resilience but also the profound difference it makes in your life and in the lives of those you touch.

Your friend,
John C. Maxwell

INTRODUCTION

I was first asked to talk about resilience with corporate audiences at the height of the Great Recession in 2008. With so much downsizing and economic upheaval during those years, it wasn't surprising that nearly every organization that invited me to speak requested a message on resilience. Still, I expected people's interest in this topic to eventually subside. But even now, I'm asked to talk about this subject more than any other. Looking back, is it any wonder?

Massive change and pressures continued unabated after that financial crisis. The proliferation of smartphones, artificial intelligence, and other technology resulted in more anxiety and less connection, faith, and trust in institutions. A global pandemic—along with the political, economic, racial, and social upheaval that followed—has stretched and stressed us all. And of course, beyond these collective stressors, each of us has our own personal journey, filled with hopes and dreams, disappointments and challenges that require resilience to navigate. Now take a moment to consider: What are your biggest challenges? Your hopes? Your worries? In what areas do you want to be more resilient? Whatever your answers, the goal of this book is to give you tools to navigate them successfully.

Resilience equips you to thrive, lead, and succeed in a world of change and uncertainty. Resilience makes you a better problem solver and confident decision-maker, not to mention a more adaptable, relaxed, and insightful person. Your ability to be effective in the face of adversity, challenges, and change depends on it.

As I studied what makes people flourish, especially in the midst of challenges, I discovered that it often boils down to a difference in their thinking. The most successful and resilient people have a way of framing their problems so that they're empowered to solve or work around challenges. They also have an approach to success that embraces passion, hope, and optimism. These thinking patterns are not tangible, so others often overlook the pivotal points where these people could have given up or failed irreparably.

With this difference in mind, I began asking myself one question while coaching clients and myself through challenges over the years:

What if there was a set of simple rules that could coach you to find an answer to any challenge you're dealing with?

My goal is to share the answer I discovered and to equip you to face any challenge by coaching you—again and again—in the right direction.

As we journey through these pages, I will help you assess your level of resilience; teach you a practical, research-based framework to help you move past obstacles; and share the personal rules that most successful people embrace to bounce back and navigate the myriad challenges of life and work. I share stories from friends and clients, including a Grammy-winning member of one of the bestselling music groups of all time, a podcaster who set out to attract three hundred listeners a week and landed over a million in her first month, and a four-time Olympian who overcame the odds in sports and used her resilience skills to beat a highly fatal form of cancer. I also include stories from my own life, family, and business.

In this book, I'll show you exactly what you need to know and do in order to build and sustain a level of resilience that empowers you to survive—and even thrive—as you navigate the challenges of your life and work.

Resilience Training Came in the Nick of Time

I first studied resilience while studying applied positive psychology in graduate school at the University of Pennsylvania. Dr. Karen Reivich, one of my professors, had researched and written extensively on resilience, and soon I began to apply what I learned from her and other positive psychology researchers to my own life. My capstone project on how high-achieving people think later became the bestselling book *Successful Women Think Differently: 9 Habits to Make You Happier, Healthier, and More Resilient*. That's also when I began delivering keynotes and workshops on resilience for corporate and government clients, ministries, and events.

Not long after, I was invited to speak on resilience, both in the United States and abroad. Dr. Marty Seligman, my former professor and a world-renowned expert in positive psychology, invited me to become a facilitator in a new resilience program being developed by the University of Pennsylvania for the US Army as a part of their Comprehensive Soldier Fitness program. I accepted, excited that my upbringing in a military family, along with my positive psychology background and speaking experience, could be helpful.

My involvement in that program could not have come at a better time for me personally. My marriage of six years had just ended, and I had moved from Maryland to Georgia to start my life over and continue to grow my business. Though I had family scattered around the Atlanta metro area where I'd settled, I worked from home, coaching clients virtually and traveling for speaking engagements. Being part of a team that taught resilience was a welcome change, and even more importantly, the subject matter reinforced the skills and habits I especially needed in that season of my life. I did it for less than a year, but the exposure and experience reshaped my life and work.

Today, in addition to writing and speaking, I am a Master Certified Coach and founder of The Coaching and Positive Psychology (CaPP) Institute, a company that trains personal and executive coaches worldwide.[1] I have the privilege of serving as one of five mentors to more than 55,000 Maxwell Leadership Certified Team members across the globe in over 100 countries, where my role is teaching coaching skills to team members. Over the past two decades, I've written thirteen other books and coached thousands of people. Enabling people to adapt to change and seize opportunities is at the heart of everything I do. And I'm not alone.

In fact, organizational psychology researchers advocate that businesses look beyond financial and human capital when seeking to solve issues around morale and adaptability. Investing in people's psychological capital—their reserves of resilience, hope, efficacy, and optimism—is one way to equip them to bounce back from setbacks and take advantage of new opportunities.[2] Without psychological capital, organizations cannot be agile enough to embrace change, adjust to growth and new technologies, or thrive in a dynamic and diverse environment. Preparing individuals to weather and thrive through challenges is so important, in fact, that I am an avid proponent of teaching resilience as a subject in every school and offering training in resilience within every organization.

Rules Are Meant to Be Chosen

After more than two decades of studying and teaching resilience, I've learned what distinguishes those who thrive in the face of the unexpected. Now I've boiled down the practical and research-based principles into a set of simple, easy-to-use rules. And if you use them regularly, both in the big challenges of life and the everyday stuff, you'll find yourself getting better, stronger, and wiser in every way. You'll have breakthroughs in your relationships, immediate shifts in your energy and motivation, and insights about how to move forward in the most meaningful ways.

Before I share the ten rules of resilience, I'll lay a foundation in the first chapter by helping you assess where you fall within the four levels of resilience and introducing you to the three pillars that support personal resilience—a combination of adaptive skills, protective resources, and preventive choices. By intentionally strengthening each of these pillars, you'll discover that challenges are easier to navigate and positive outcomes are more frequent.

Each of the ten chapters that follow will introduce you to a practical, easy-to-remember rule that provides specific guidance on overcoming challenges. The more you practice the rules, the more they will become a part of your mindset and the faster you will find the wisest way forward, bounce back from setbacks and challenges, and seize new opportunities. Depending on the dilemma or challenge you face, you can decide which rule applies best in any given situation. The "bonus" rule you'll learn about in the final chapter will challenge you to offer what you've learned to others in a way that will enrich your life and theirs.

Along the way, I'll share inspiring, relatable stories from those who've found tremendous success in the face of improbable odds. These stories demonstrate the rules of resilience in action. You'll notice coaching prompts throughout each chapter that are designed to help you think differently and more productively. A Try This experiment at the end of each chapter is another coaching tool to help you try out new ideas and actions to determine what works best for you.

Let me explain what I mean when I use the term *coaching*. Coaching is helping someone move from where they are to where they really want to be, and to navigate the challenges and opportunities that appear along the way. One of the first things I teach my clients is that answering powerful questions can shift us in ways that give us the insight and strength to keep going. Pausing to do so is a form of resilience.

Coaching has been the most important tool I have used at pivotal points in my life to get unstuck and gain wisdom and clarity about next steps and how to take them. Both coaching and self-coaching are resilience tools. Self-coaching is the process of pausing intentionally, reflecting on the challenge you wish to navigate, and asking and honestly answering thought-provoking questions that can reveal the answers and actions that empower resilience. My goal in this book is not only to serve as your coach, but to give you the tools to self-coach. The self-coaching questions throughout this book will lead you to wiser, deeper, and faster answers to any dilemma. Practicing the skill of self-coaching will help you draw on the rules of resilience to solve problems more quickly, seize opportunities confidently, and gain insights that strengthen your well-being, success, and happiness.

I believe wholeheartedly in these rules because I've lived them. I've coached others who've used them. I've studied why they work. When I get stuck now, it's because I've momentarily forgotten to embrace these principles. At points when I needed them most, these rules have pulled me through. And I know they can work for you, your team, and your family. I believe that if we all collectively practice them, we will inspire others to be more resilient, too, creating a more resilient world.

I'm excited and honored to walk alongside you on this journey. I invite you to return to these pages again and again, taking away just what you need for any challenge you face now and in the future. Let's get started!

Your friend and coach,

Valorie Burton

CREATE AND CULTIVATE A PERSONAL SYSTEM OF RESILIENCE

Why you have more control over your resilience than you might think

---

KEY MESSAGES

- Resilience is key to navigating challenges and maximizing opportunities.
- Intentionally build your "personal resilience system" on three powerful pillars.
- Evaluate your current resilience level.

Whatever made you pick up this book, my guess is that you have already been resilient in many ways. And you understand that knowledge can mean the difference between success or failure, whether the challenge you face right now is in a relationship, your career, your health, or your finances. Over the years, clients have rarely come to me saying, "I want more resilience," but that is ultimately the goal all of them have had in common.

For example, Danielle, a trailblazing businesswoman, got the unexpected call to interview with a former president of the United States for a position on his team and used our coaching to help her navigate that opportunity successfully. Robin, a savvy attorney who longed for marriage and motherhood, lost an IVF pregnancy at forty-six and wanted help reimagining her future.

James, an educator who overcame terrible abuse at the hands of his mother as a child, needed help—at work and with family—to learn to speak up, set boundaries, and be happy. And Jamal, who is amazing at pretty much everything, longed to stop letting imposter syndrome and perfectionism get the best of him so he could finally gain the confidence to step out in faith and pursue his most authentic goals.

Like these clients, I bet you, too, have endured many situations in which you needed resilience, even if that's not the word you might have used to describe it. When we are resilient, we are tapping into rules that we can intentionally use again and again to navigate any challenge that comes along. These rules are rooted in three powerful pillars that form the foundation for your personal system of resilience. So that's where I want us to start, even before we dive into the rules. But first, let's consider the term *resilience*.

What Is Resilience?

Resilience is most often described as the ability to bounce back and successfully navigate challenges, adversity, and change. The American Psychological Association defines resilience as "the process and outcome of successfully adapting to difficult or challenging life experiences, especially through mental, emotional and behavioral flexibility and adjustment to external and internal demands."[1]

That definition is accurate. In this book, though, I invite you to see your resilience more importantly as a *system* you create that enables you to adapt to, withstand, and recover from stressors. A system is an organized framework or method—a set of rules, choices, or procedures that accomplish a specific goal. In this case, the goal is resilience, which is a necessary ingredient for success. The stronger your system of resilience, the more likely you are to accomplish a vision or overcome hardship and setbacks.

ASK YOURSELF

What would greater resilience in your life enable you to do?

Notice that resilience not only puts you in the best situation to withstand stress, but it also positions you to seize opportunities. It is not just about overcoming difficulties or minimizing their impact, but multiplying the good like compound interest. Success requires resilience, not only because the path to accomplishment is often filled with obstacles and unexpected challenges, but because the rules of resilience lay the groundwork that makes success easier to attain and sustain.

Three Supporting Pillars

If resilience is a system, how do you build a strong foundation to support it? You begin by taking personal ownership of your life and work by intentionally setting yourself up to deal with challenges and grasp opportunities when they come.

In 2015, a multidisciplinary group of scientists consolidated the existing research on factors that lead to resilience in children. The resulting report helped me identify the three elements, or pillars, that are key to overcoming obstacles and seizing opportunities at any age: adaptive skills, protective resources, and preventive measures.[2] Each rule in this book reflects one or more of these pillars. Just know that as you intentionally build and cultivate each pillar, your resilience will get stronger and stronger. By considering each of these pillars on its own, you can easily evaluate your resilience level. You can tell where you are strong and where you are weak, and make wise choices about what steps to take to increase your resilience. Seeing resilience as a system with three distinct pillars is a practical way for you to identify opportunities for growth and act in ways that produce real and positive change.

FIRST PILLAR: ADAPTIVE SKILLS

Adaptive skills are about how you think, react, and behave in response to challenges and opportunities. They determine the energy you bring to problem-solving as well as help formulate your strategy as you respond to adversity and opportunity. Adaptive skills are the inner resources that involve your mental, emotional, and spiritual states.

These skills are somewhat invisible and intangible because they are developed internally through your thoughts, motivations, and approach to life. They can be learned and honed through awareness and practice. Consider the challenges for which you most need resilience in this season as you look at the factors that make up adaptive skills:

- responsibility and personal ownership
- thought awareness
- optimistic mindset and thinking style
- goal setting and planning
- locus of control
- strength leveraging
- positive emotion
- energy maintenance and management
- self-coaching
- flexibility
- self-compassion
- faith
- hope and optimism
- authenticity and humility

If you have dealt with a fair number of challenges, you've likely developed adaptive skills over time through necessity. If you have been shielded from or spared adversity in life and work, you may not have had the opportunity to learn or practice these adaptive skills. And even if you've faced some difficulties, new challenges that require levels of resilience you've never had to muster may still crop up.

As we look at the rules of resilience, we will delve further into what these skills entail, and why and how you can acquire and build them into your life and work to increase your resilience. You may already have an excellent grasp of some of these skills while you may need to hone others. You may not have even considered these as resilience skills, but I hope you'll gain an appreciation as to why they matter and how they can transform your ability to navigate challenges and reach your vision in any situation.

People's adaptive skills are not always apparent until you observe how they process and interpret the situations they are faced with. The most resilient people think differently—but their thoughts aren't always obvious.

SECOND PILLAR: PROTECTIVE RESOURCES

Protective resources tend to be more tangible and visible than adaptive skills. Typically, you can point to, name, and see these resources, which may include positive, supportive relationships; physical security; money; or access to services. Sometimes they are yours by virtue of the family, community, or even country you were born into. Not all protective resources come to us in this way, but many of them do. This is important because it helps us see how resilience can, in part, result from circumstances that are not of your own doing. But if you don't have them by the good fortune of happenstance, you can intentionally build these resources over time.

They are called protective resources because they can shield you from the damaging effects of stressors. When thinking of these resources, you may think of money first. But in the context of resilience, resources refer to anything tangible that protects you from the negative impacts of adversity, as well as anything that makes it easier to navigate challenges. These can include

- financial and work resources
- education and training
- experience
- environment
- health
- access to resources
- supportive relationships

Supportive relationships may be the most significant of the protective resources, so we will consider how to rally your relationships in Rule #5.

THIRD PILLAR: PREVENTIVE MEASURES

The third pillar, preventive measures, reduces and lessens the impact of adversity. Preventive measures are about thinking ahead and taking care of your future self. It is the skill of stepping into the shoes of your future self and asking, *What will I wish I had done?* Whatever you answer usually leads you to the best choice to make in the present.

These proactive choices, in other words, reduce your risk for adversity. This is the wisdom of foresight and discipline that often comes with experience. You carry forward new approaches to life and work that emerge as you triumph over stressors, empowering you to avoid or minimize similar challenges in the future.

For example, your future self might thank you tomorrow because you are well-rested for a big day after making the decision to go to bed early and get a good and full night's sleep. Or years from now you may be grateful to yourself because you started consistently investing for your future early on. Some challenges are beyond our control, but putting yourself in the best position to withstand potential challenges is what preventive measures are all about. It's wisdom in action.

A fascinating example of the power of preventive measures comes from the field of medicine. The 2019 influenza vaccine offered protection against two A-strain flu viruses and two B-strain viruses. It was what is called a quadrivalent vaccine because it targeted the four most common strains of flu. One of those B strains, Yamagata, has not been detected since March 2020. You probably recognize that as the month the World Health Organization declared COVID-19 to be not just an epidemic but a global pandemic. In an effort to minimize the spread of the disease, the use of masks, social distancing, and increased handwashing became the norm. These changes in behavior, while aimed at containing COVID, also rendered the Yamagata strain of the flu extinct. By 2024, vaccine scientists at the Food and Drug Administration declared that protection against the Yamagata strain was no longer needed and asked vaccine manufacturers to drop it from production, making the flu vaccine a trivalent flu vaccine, targeting just three strains.[3] Not only that, but the preventive measures against COVID-19 led flu deaths to plummet. During a particularly virulent year in 2017–2018, more than 51,000 people in the United States died of influenza. The number of deaths dropped more than 50 percent in 2019–2020 and then by 90 percent during the 2021–2022 flu season. But once the pandemic ended and preventive measures tapered off, flu deaths crept back up again.[4]

In essence, simple preventive measures significantly reduced the occurrence of the challenge, and therefore dramatically lowered the number of deaths—even eliminating one strain of the flu entirely. Now imagine how preventive measures could work in your own life to reduce the risk of preventable adversities and challenges.

Although we cannot predict or control which stressors will come our way, preventive measures can minimize and even eliminate the likelihood of certain challenges. We can be intentional about putting ourselves in the best position to overcome those challenges when they arise. The most successful people are adept at clearing their path of unnecessary stressors and adversities. You can make choices and build your life and work in such a way that you set yourself up for success.

Tipping the Scales

Of course, we can never entirely eliminate challenges and adversity. They're part of the human experience. And stress, in and of itself, is not a bad thing. Much like germs and bacteria build a baby's immune system, some amount of stress strengthens your resilience system, giving you the opportunity to step out of your comfort zone, grow, build your mental muscles, and even inspire you to improve and perform better. Stress also increases alertness and memory, and it helps you focus your energy to get things done. It is prolonged and overwhelming stress that is harmful. Chronic, heavy stress is what you want to avoid—negative drama in ongoing relationships, continual financial strain, unrelenting health challenges, years of struggling in a career or business, and any threats to your well-being.

This is where adaptive skills, protective resources, and preventive measures, amassed over time, can begin to create a new reality with more joy and peace, and less stress and adversity. When your resources outweigh the stressors you face, the resilience scale tips toward positive outcomes. But when stressors outweigh your adaptive skills and resources, the opposite occurs.[5]

This scale illustrates the concept that resilience is a system we create that positions us to weather storms and to seize opportunities.

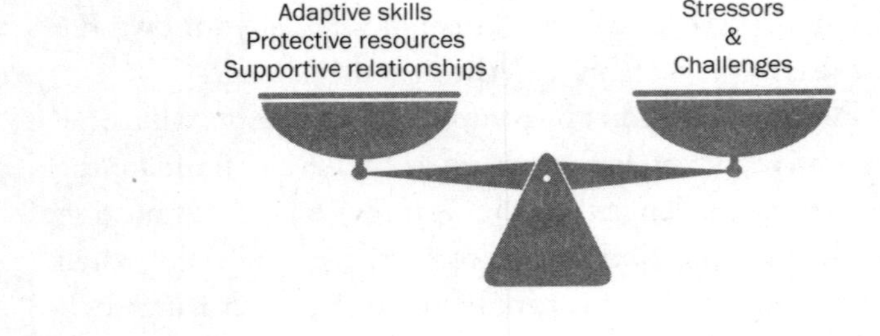

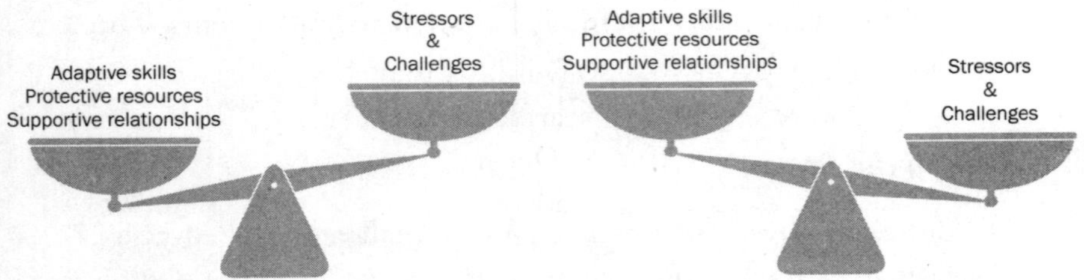

When the resources outweigh the stressors, you are resilient.

When the stressors outweigh the resources, you are not resilient.

If you intentionally learn adaptive skills like thought awareness, nurture protective resources such as supportive relationships, and prepare for future challenges by taking preventive measures, you will build a personal system of resilience. In fact, you may discover that success often finds its way to you even when you aren't looking.

Psychologists can often predict who will be more resilient in certain situations just by observing these three factors. For example, having even one stable, helpful, and committed relationship is critical, not just to build resilience in children, but also to support resilience in adults.[6] Think back on a significant challenge you overcame. It is likely that someone influenced your ability to conquer the challenge, whether through their encouragement, helpful actions, or information they shared. Maybe it was their consistent belief in you or their example, which modeled for you how to move through the challenge effectively. While children, by virtue of their vulnerability, may have a greater need for supportive relationships, adults rely heavily on the support systems around them too. The more aware you are of this truth, the more purposeful you can be about welcoming positive relationships into your life while building and tapping into them. You'll become more intentional about seeking wise counsel, coaching, and advice, and using that wisdom to protect, build, and enhance your life, as well as to identify potential blind spots that could derail your plans.

Here's an example of what I mean. When my father was fifty-four, he sought out a new primary care physician after moving from Colorado to northern Virginia. During a routine physical, his new doctor noticed that my dad's heartbeat was irregular. It wasn't the first time he had been told this. During annual checkups throughout his military career, my dad had been told he had this condition, but no one ever suggested further testing. My father was otherwise quite healthy, and his doctors didn't seem concerned. Occasionally, a medical professional would point out that some people just have irregular heartbeats or murmurs.

But this doctor's response was different. He was curious and wanted to understand why the heartbeat was irregular. He told my dad, "I just want us to find out the reason behind it to make sure there is nothing we need to be concerned about."

The physician ordered an angiogram, medical imaging used to visualize the arteries, veins, and heart chambers. Typically, the test is used to detect blockages in the arteries caused by the buildup of cholesterol, fat, and other substances. I went with my father to the hospital for the procedure, and I'll never forget the cardiologist's words after they wheeled him to a private room after the angiogram.

"Well, I have good news and bad news," the cardiologist began. Dad and I looked at the doctor wide-eyed and then at each other, anxiously bracing for the bad news. "The good news is that your arteries are in perfect condition! No blockages whatsoever," he explained. We smiled tentatively, relieved by that news but perplexed by what the bad news might be if his arteries were so healthy.

"The bad news is that one of your arteries is going to the wrong place," the cardiologist said. "You have a rare birth defect. Most people born with this condition die by six months, but certainly by the age of ten."

We couldn't believe what we were hearing. The physician continued. "All the doctors are buzzing around the floor talking about your case. We've not seen anyone live this long with your condition. You need open heart surgery as soon as possible to correct it."

We were stunned. "You could walk up and down the streets of Manhattan all day and not find another person with this problem," the doctor went on. My dad looked contemplative, but also had a grin on his face, as he processed what the cardiologist had just said.

I later learned the grin was a sign of gratitude. "I'm blessed to even be alive," he told me. While he'd had the condition his entire life, no one had ever sent him for further testing. The concern and support of his new primary care physician may have prolonged my father's life by ten to fifteen years, according to the cardiologist. That primary care physician was a protective resource in my father's life, providing critical information. It also made him stronger and healthier. Once he recovered, he told me he could feel that his body was getting much more oxygen. His energy and stamina increased noticeably during workouts.

But in addition to this protective resource, my dad also benefited from preventive measures he'd put in place long ago. Before the cardiologist left the room, Dad asked him, "Why do you think I beat the odds and lived just fine all these years? I've never even suspected I had a heart defect. I played sports growing up. I retired after twenty-four years in the Air Force with no physical problems."

The cardiologist explained that my dad had likely thrived *because* of those factors. "Your healthy lifestyle is probably what saved you," the doctor told him. "Otherwise, you might have had a heart attack at a young age, and no one ever would have known about the heart defect. They would have just said it was a fluke."

In other words, the preventive measures of strong health—exercise, no smoking, healthy weight—may have tipped the resilience scale in my father's favor. My dad also drew on strong adaptive skills—an optimistic outlook, faith, a good sense of humor, and other healthy coping skills. Research shows that positive emotions and a belief in a power greater than yourself are predictors of resilience and longevity.[7]

Of course, my father didn't spend his life strengthening these three pillars because he knew that a positive outlook, good health, and a conscientious physician could prevent him from having a heart attack due to an undiagnosed heart defect. Nonetheless, controlling the factors he could ultimately helped him weather an unexpected silent storm. He built a system of resilience that for years withstood a major physical stressor.

What Is Your *Level of Resilience?*

How do you know if you are resilient in a particular area? Resilience can truly be measured only when you see how you manage a stressor under pressure. While it's easy to categorize people and groups as being either resilient or not, it's also helpful to think of levels of resilience. Consider these four levels as you evaluate your own resilience. Think of an area right now where you need more resilience. Perhaps it is in your career or business, a relationship or health situation. Then look at the illustration below.

Resilience can truly be measured only when you see how you manage a stressor under pressure.

1—Thriving

2—Functioning (surviving, but not thriving)

3—Malfunctioning (struggling)

4—Nonfunctioning (broken, permanently failing)

Anything above the line represents some degree of resilience, ranging from functioning or surviving to actually thriving. When you face a challenge and are functioning, that simply means that you are surviving or recovering from the setback and maintaining your level of well-being, productivity, or effectiveness. Thriving means you are doing even better than before, perhaps showing little evidence of the stressor's impact on your well-being, productivity, or effectiveness. At the highest level of thriving, the setback may have in some way positively impacted you, opened a new and advantageous door of opportunity, or accelerated your growth, well-being, and success.

Anything below the line represents being "unresilient." And yes, I know that's technically not a word, but it is the most direct way to describe a lack of resilience, so let's make it one. *Unresilient* is the opposite of resilient—a term that is simple and clear. It describes someone who is unable to successfully adapt to challenging life experiences and lacks a personal system that enables them to withstand, adapt, and recover from stressors.

When you are unresilient, the stressor has taken a heavy toll. You may be struggling to adapt, proactively take responsibility, or grow in ways that help you be resilient. At the lowest level, you may utterly fail in a situation and be unable to bounce back. The situation appears irreparable. This is the friendship that never mends or the marriage that lands in divorce court. It's the financial situation that leads to bankruptcy or the career that goes up in smoke. It is the person who gives up and languishes, never realizing their own potential.

The good news is this: No matter how you rate your level of resilience today, you can make it stronger.

Too often, when we doubt our ability to make it through a challenge, we don't push back enough. When a seemingly rhetorical question arises, we don't answer it. But success—whether in relationships, business, health, or finances—is impossible without the ability to navigate the inevitable obstacles and challenges that arise. And overcoming doubts means answering the questions that trigger our biggest fears and suspicions that we can't do it, can't make it, or somehow don't have what it takes.

Remember that the things worth doing are often *hard*. That's because changing is hard. Stepping out of our comfort zone is hard. Dealing with the unexpected and with disappointment is hard. Disappointment can drain us of the will to hope for something better. Even changes we want can be hard. And while sometimes we have to deal with big, devastating challenges, nearly every day we deal with the small but persistent ones: the need to be at our best at work and at home, to manage our eating and spending habits, and to deal with difficult people, traffic, and the world at large without becoming overstressed or overwhelmed. These challenges accumulate over time and test our ability to push through the hard things.

Simply by reading this book, however, you are taking an important first step. The rules of resilience offer an approach to handling your challenges and opportunities so that you are in the best position to conquer whatever comes your way. These rules will also help you build a strong foundation that gives you the best chance to thrive personally and professionally.

Coach Yourself

- If you are completely honest right now, what is your current resilience level in each of these areas? (Remember, 1 = thriving, 2 = functioning/surviving, 3 = malfunctioning, and 4 = non-functioning.)

  _____ relationships

  _____ finances

  _____ work/business

  _____ health

  _____ spiritual life

  _____ additional areas

- Identify a specific challenge in your life today that you would like to approach with greater resilience.

- In the challenge that most needs your resilience right now, what do you want your resilience level to be? (Note: You have permission to simply aspire to make it through your challenge intact!)

- Consider for a moment the three pillars of resilience: adaptive skills, protective resources, and preventive measures.

  For each pillar, notice which attributes you already possess.

  Which pillar is strongest for you?

  Which pillar is weakest, and therefore offers you the biggest opportunity to strengthen your resilience?

Try This

- ☐ Review the three pillars and identify a step you can take to strengthen your weakest pillar.
- ☐ Decide when you'll take the step, how you'll move forward, and who can help you stay accountable.
- ☐ Consider your current level of resilience. What would it take to move up a level?

SAY IT WITH ME:

"Resilience enables me to overcome obstacles and optimize opportunities."

RESILIENCE RULE #1

EXPECT THE UNEXPECTED

How a small dose of pessimism will help you build a personal foundation of resilience that empowers you to thrive through your challenges

---

KEY MESSAGES

- Don't just think positively, think accurately.
- Accept that changes and challenges are part of life.
- Look for ways to strengthen your pillars so you're ready for unexpected opportunities.

From my home in Annapolis, Maryland, I drove south on I-95 in my sienna red BMW Z3 convertible with the top down. Devastated that my marriage was on the brink of divorce, I was driving to Anderson, South Carolina, to return to my safe place, my mother's home. I needed time and space to think. I'd turned thirty-six just a couple of months earlier, and while my career as an author, coach, and speaker was unfolding as I'd hoped, my personal life was falling apart. The story I'd imagined for my life included being happily married and raising children, but that was not my reality. Quite the opposite. I was *unhappily* married with *no* children. It's not exactly the way I had expected my life to unfold.

If it were up to you and me, we wouldn't need resilience. Success would be an easy destination, and we would achieve it free of annoying obstacles like disappointment, difficult people, and everyday challenges. Better yet, we would never experience negative events, the loss of people and things we love, or unfulfilled dreams. Instead, success would unfold just as we imagine it. And the road map to our dream job, dream body, dream bank account, and dream relationship would be a short, straight line between points A and B. But we all know that's not how it works. That's why you and I are meeting on the pages of this book.

Getting to the good stuff almost always means enduring some not-so-good stuff—stuff you'd rather not have to deal with and circumstances you wish didn't exist. And if you want to not just survive it but even to thrive in spite of it, you need some rules to live by. Easy to remember. Immediate in impact. And timeless. These rules are about ensuring your well-being and success as you face both opportunities and challenges.

"Expect the unexpected" is the foundational rule of resilience because it is inevitable that challenges will arise. The first rule of resilience is to anticipate these challenges and prepare to (1) prevent them in the first place, (2) cushion the blow the stressor brings, and (3) recover from the stressor as completely and efficiently as possible. This first rule of resilience is a commitment to remembering that change and challenges are a constant. Therefore, it is wise to prepare for them, knowing they will interrupt your best-laid plans.

A famous failure from the world of aviation illuminates the power of the first rule of resilience. In 1949, the United States Air Force sought to understand the possibilities and limits of new aviation technology. Dr. John Stapp, a US Air Force officer, flight surgeon, and biophysicist, oversaw much of the research, including experimentation using a rocket sled that could reach supersonic speeds. Often he made himself the test pilot on these G-force experiments because of the risk involved. Before one of the tests, Captain Edward Murphy asked an assistant to wire four electronic gauges to shoulder straps that Stapp would wear for an experiment designed to measure the impact of supersonic flight speeds and crashes on the human body. The assistant did as he was told, but when the test concluded, the sensors provided zero data. Every single one had failed.

Perplexed by the problem, Captain Murphy quickly discovered

that all four gauges had been wired backward when they were built. Frustrated because it wasn't the first time something had gone ridiculously wrong on the project, and disgusted by the lack of attention to detail, Captain Murphy was said to have uttered pessimistically, "If there's any way these guys can do it wrong, they will."[1]

Shortly after, Dr. Stapp was interviewed by a reporter who wanted to know how the Air Force had avoided injuries and fatalities with such a dangerous set of experiments. Stapp explained that they anticipated many possible failures and worst-case scenarios, and then prepared for them before anyone could get hurt. He explained to the reporter that his team operated under "Murphy's Law, if anything can go wrong, it will." Today, we often hear Murphy's Law described with an expanded caveat, "If anything can go wrong, it will, and at the worst possible moment."

This maxim may sound pessimistic, and that's because it is. Research shows that this type of pessimism is exactly the sort of outlook that empowers success, especially in the face of improbable odds. When you expect obstacles, you have a more realistic assessment of what it will take to actually meet your goal. The most successful people use pessimism to evaluate and plan effectively but then tap into optimism, knowing that positive action and perseverance will lead to favorable results. In fact, this combination of positive yet accurate thinking is the basis of this first rule of resilience: "Expect the unexpected."

Maybe Murphy's Law sounds a little over the top. Is it really true that if anything can go wrong, it will? I mean, sometimes nothing goes wrong. But I have found that even on my best-planned road trip, I am likely to encounter a traffic jam, rainstorm, or need for more pit stops than I expected. Your life's journey is akin to a road trip. It is wise to approach life with the assumption that something likely will not go as planned and that the best policy is to be prepared—or at least unsurprised when the unforeseen happens. Expecting everything to go as planned is a setup for disappointment.

If you've ever had your plans disrupted by events you didn't anticipate, you know the frustration of unexpected or unwelcome hurdles.

Expecting everything to go as planned is a setup for disappointment.

Sometimes, though, it's not even the unexpected that throws us off course. If we are honest, sometimes the hurdles we must clear are predictable, but we still weren't ready for them. The expectation that obstacles should not or will not appear is one of the biggest threats to resilience. This is because if you don't expect complications, you won't prepare for or try to prevent them from happening in the first place.

If you expect the unexpected, you prepare as though it is inevitable. You put yourself in the best position to weather a storm, bounce back quickly, and even fail forward when possible, coming out ahead of where you would have been if the detour had not been necessary.

To be clear, resilience isn't needed just for negative events and stressors; it's needed for the positive ones too. When you get a promotion or start a new business, it may be exciting, but it's also a major change that can create stress and the risk of mistakes or failure. The same is true when you get married, have a child, or move across the world to pursue a lifelong dream. One of the most notorious examples of needing resilience after a positive life event is landing a windfall of cash. Of those who win the lottery, approximately one-third file for bankruptcy within three to five years.[2] In comparison, only about 12 percent of people have filed for bankruptcy at some point in their lives.[3] Sudden fortune requires resilience to navigate, as it can be a major change that requires good decision-making, planning, self-control, and perhaps mentors who can support wise choices to preserve newfound wealth over time. It requires a system that supports success.

What Do You Want to Be Ready For?

If I could open a door of opportunity for you right now, what would you be stepping into? Whether it's a promotion or business venture, the relationship you hope for, or anything else you dream of, resilience means being ready to seize the chance when it presents itself. Sometimes you may be offered a sudden positive opportunity that requires the resilience to pivot on a dime because there is no time for preparation—you need to already be ready.

An amazing example of someone who was prepared for an unexpected, incredible opportunity is Tenitra Michelle Williams, who seamlessly stepped into the chart-topping musical group Destiny's Child in 2000 after the sudden and infamous exit of two of its original members. Michelle and I met a few years ago as we connected around our work of writing and speaking about mental health and personal growth, and we became friends. She's also a graduate of The CaPP Institute, earning her designation from us as a Certified Personal and Executive Coach while simultaneously rehearsing and performing in a Broadway musical! Talk about focus—she has it. The first time we sat down for lunch, I immediately sensed her intelligence, humility, and authentic confidence. Her sense of humor and transparency are evident whenever she shares her struggles and faith-filled triumphs in an effort to inspire others.

The lead-up to her unexpected rise in the spotlight started in the late nineties. After two years at Illinois State University, she decided to pause her studies for the chance tour as a backup singer with Grammy-winning R&B star Monica.

"We toured and went to Japan with TLC," she remembers. The tour was a big deal, but Michelle took it in stride. A duet from Monica's second album had spent a record-breaking thirteen weeks at number one on the Billboard charts.[4] It was a dynamic experience for a nineteen-year-old criminal justice major who did a little singing on the side.

When the tour ended, Michelle expected to go back to school, grateful for what she assumed had been "a nice little opportunity." But deep down, she discerned that she should perhaps stay open to one more gig. She wasn't planning on a music career, but she was confident of her singing abilities and had enjoyed the experience of touring.

"At the time, I was aiming to be an amazing prosecuting attorney or a forensic psychologist," she says. "Music was a hobby for me because I just didn't see myself doing music at that level. I knew I was talented, but my mom was pro-education, pro-401(k), pro-health and dental, and pro-paycheck every two weeks! Why would you choose a career where you might be paid today and then not get paid again?" she adds, explaining her mom's career advice. It made sense, and she planned to follow that advice—but first, maybe she'd land just one more fun backup opportunity if she had the chance.

"I said, 'Mom, if you let me do one more gig, I'm going to get you that Chrysler 300M,'" she recalls of their conversation, laughing at her strategy to get her mom's approval. "She loved those cars back then."

Rather than the background engagement she hoped for, she got a call from an acquaintance who suggested Michelle talk to Tina Knowles, Beyoncé's mother, as a possible replacement for a Destiny's Child member who was leaving the group. Michelle says she spoke to Ms. Knowles over the phone and then flew to audition for the group. She sang one of her favorite hymns, "Blessed Assurance," for them. It was an authentic and bold choice of an audition song for a group whose first number one hit—"Bills, Bills, Bills"—had recently topped the Billboard Hot 100, but it was a choice true to her gospel roots. The rest is history.

Destiny's Child founding members Beyoncé Knowles and Kelly Rowland loved it and invited Michelle to join the group in early 2000. It was a strategic and high-profile change to a four-member group whose bestselling second album had been released only months earlier. Two other group members had just exited after much-publicized turmoil.

Everything in Michelle's life changed immediately. She pivoted from backup singer and college student to member of one of the best-known groups of the era. She had to rely on her preparation since childhood, which she says gave her maturity beyond her years. In addition to singing as long as she could remember, Michelle had also directed the adult choir at church from the age of twelve, choosing the songs and accompanying Scriptures, learning all three parts, and teaching each section of the choir their part. She knew music. And of course, she had been a part of a major international tour as a backup singer.

"They knew they didn't have time to train anybody. There were video shoots already scheduled. There were tours in place. It wasn't a group that was in development. They had already sold millions of records," she explains of the unusual opportunity. She was ready, and the group took off in an even bigger way with chart-toppers like "Survivor" and "Independent Women Part 1," the theme song from the film *Charle's Angels*, cementing their iconic place in music. Destiny's Child became one of the bestselling American female groups of all time, second only to TLC. The success of the group opened the door for Michelle's award-winning solo career as a gospel artist and a prolific acting career spanning more than two decades, primarily on Broadway in *Aida*, *Chicago*, and *Once on This Island*, and in the traveling national tour of *The Color Purple*. She also originated the role of Viola Van Horn in the comedy *Death Becomes Her*.

The thing about unexpected opportunities is that sometimes they come with a new set of challenges. The exciting opportunity that changed everything for Michelle also came with unexpected stressors and criticism. "Sometimes it's best not to know everything. It's best to just know you've got what it takes," she says of her early days with Destiny's Child. She did her best to stay focused on that thought as she found her footing in the group and with fans who were skeptical of the change.

"The other members already had fans who loved them, and then here I come in, like, 'Hi! I'm their replacement!' These folks don't know me at all. I was a surprise [to the fans]. I was a surprise to the other two that left. It was like, 'What? Who's this?'" she recalls.

As exciting as her whirlwind new career was, Michelle was filled with insecurities early on. She had to find a way to deal with them, or this opportunity might have slipped through her fingers. Incidentally, she wasn't the only new replacement. The other singer, however, left after five months with the group. Destiny's Child, who'd had four members for years, decided to become a trio with Michelle as the sole new member. She says it took time to feel accepted, and she had to come to terms with that. At times, it was hard to feel confident when she walked into a room with Kelly and Beyoncé because she knew not everyone would embrace her. Ultimately the two women who'd chosen her gave her the confidence she needed as she worked through her feelings. "B and Kelly were like, 'We want you in this group! Let's go!'"

Together they were on a mission, she said. Shifting her focus to the sisterhood they formed and the vision they shared helped. "We were focused on success, not just a cute little song. No, we wanted to be one of the greatest groups of all time."

When we consider Michelle Williams's need for resilience in the face of an unexpected, exciting opportunity, it's clear that her story reflects all three pillars of resilience as she followed the foundational rule, "Expect the unexpected." She used adaptive skills such as authenticity while auditioning in a way that reflected her strengths and beliefs. She didn't try to be who she thought they wanted. She chose to show up as herself. Once in the group, she was aware of her thoughts and noticed what she was saying to herself about the criticism, which wasn't helpful. So she intentionally focused on embracing the support of her fellow members, Kelly Rowland and Beyoncé, rather than listening to the initial mixed reactions that followed her becoming a part of the group. She used humility and authenticity to empathize with fans who already had their favorites in Destiny's Child, recognizing it wasn't personal. She accepted that it would take time for the group's fans to embrace her. And eventually they did. Her protective resources—including a close and supportive relationship with her mom and years of musical and leadership experience with her church choir—provided a secure launching pad that helped her seize the opportunity and make the most of it, parlaying it into a long-term, fulfilling career. That's a high level of career resilience—not just surviving a challenge, but thriving in it.

Whatever challenge you face, whether an unexpected, unwelcome dilemma or an unexpected, welcome surprise, you can establish or enhance these three pillars to build your own personal system of resilience. Here are some practical ways to prepare for the unexpected:

- **Shift your expectations.** When you don't expect things to always unfold as you planned, it is easier to adapt when the unexpected arrives.. Expect good things to happen, but be realistic about the possibility of the unexpected and decide in advance that no matter what happens, you can and will adapt, relying on creativity, relationships, and the resources you cultivate.

- **Pause, then plan.** When life throws you off course, you may feel a bit dizzy at first. Give yourself the space and time to process change and get your bearings. Take a breath, assess the situation, then start planning for how you can adjust, rally your resources, and meet the challenge in front of you.

- **Think ahead.** Always think about ways you can build your life so that it is more resilient in the face of challenges. From strong relationships and emergency savings to taking care of your health and equipping yourself with skills that give you career options, build a strong support system of resources that will cushion you from the unexpected challenges life can bring.

- **Manage your thoughts.** One of the most important resilience skills is thought awareness. Notice what you're saying to yourself about your challenge and whether your thoughts are moving you forward or getting you stuck. Be intentional about choosing thoughts that align with your vision and help you move in a positive direction.

Coach Yourself

- When you think of the first rule of resilience, "Expect the unexpected," in which areas of your life do you most want to increase your resilience and why?
- In what area(s) might you be unprepared for the unexpected? Consider your relationships, work, finances, and health.
- If you were to expect the unexpected, what might you do differently to prepare for or reduce the likelihood of the unexpected actually happening?
- As you consider your vision for your work or personal life, what one step could you take now to be ready for an opportunity that might unexpectedly come up?

Try This

- ☐ Set a goal for the area of resilience you want to strengthen first.
- ☐ Determine one to three steps you could take to prepare for or reduce the impact of challenges in that area.
- ☐ Identify an unexpected opportunity you would love to come your way.
- ☐ Imagine how you would handle and maximize that opportunity if that door opened.

SAY IT WITH ME:

"I expect the unexpected
and equip myself to handle it."

RESILIENCE RULE #2

CHOOSE THOUGHTS THAT STRENGTHEN YOU

Why thought awareness is the most important resilience skill of all and how you can master it

---

KEY MESSAGES

- It's not what happens that matters most; it's how you think about what happens.
- You can self-coach your way to more helpful interpretations of stressful events.
- With practice, you can rewire the patterns in your brain for greater resilience.

The morning sunlight peeked through the gap in my bedroom curtains just enough to nudge me awake. I opened my eyes reluctantly, wanting to keep them closed but feeling guilty about the idea. After all, I had work to get done. But it was a Friday and the day after a holiday, so it really wasn't a workday. Or was it? I hadn't actually decided I would take the day off, though I'd thought about it. Because I hadn't finished everything I wanted to get done during the three-day workweek, I had a to-do list hangover that was interrupting my rest.

I grabbed my watch from the nightstand and looked at the time: 8:02 a.m. It was way past my normal wake-up time. I had ignored my own no-phone-by-the-bed rule the night before, so the phone was just an arm's length away. Without even looking or thinking, my left hand reached to feel for the phone on the nightstand. I opened the screen. A neighbor had texted. They had made last-minute plans to go to the lake and wondered if our son wanted to go on a day trip with their family. It was a fun invitation. But my anxiety kicked in immediately. There is something about my son going away that leaves me catastrophizing about something going wrong. Catastrophizing is when your thoughts spiral downward as you imagine worst-case, irrational scenarios of what might go wrong. Ever done that? I cannot explain where this irrational fear comes from, but the feelings it produces are stressful and real. Rather than answering the text, I rolled back over and attempted to go to sleep. This day was already emotionally off. Guilt, anxiety, and decision fatigue were winning, and my feet had not even touched the floor yet!

It wasn't that anything earth-shattering had happened in those first few minutes of consciousness that Friday. It was small thoughts, strung together, that created a chain of negative emotions that threatened to upend what would otherwise have been a great day. Without a vision for how the day would go, I was conflicted when deciding whether to wake up and get going or enjoy some rest. With anxious, irrational thoughts flooding my mind, a time-sensitive text went unanswered while I procrastinated. Have you ever been there? That place where your thoughts leave you anxious and feeling off?

Recognizing my irrational thoughts, I decided to wake my husband, Jeff, and tell him about the invitation. He has no anxiety about such things. Before I could even say, "How should we answer?" he happily said, "That's great!" Then he hopped out of bed, woke Alex up, and got him off for a day of fun with his friend and their family. I was still catastrophizing while Jeff and Alex were downstairs making breakfast.

The one thing that soothes my anxieties when Alex goes out without us is making sure he has our extra phone with him. But somehow, in the rush to get him next door, it was left behind.

I noticed the phone he'd left on the kitchen island when Jeff and I came back inside after dropping him off. Then I glanced at the little flip calendar we keep on the counter: July 5. It's my parents' anniversary. After their divorce, I used to cry every year on this date.

But it had not upset me in nearly fifteen years. Today, though, I felt a tinge of sadness, like a gray cloud hovering over me. Could the negative start to my day have had something to do with this? The cloud hovered, and more negative thoughts drizzled through my mind. Suddenly I remembered that my assistant of four years was leaving in another week and I didn't yet have anyone to take her place. Another decision I needed to make. *I'm tired of making decisions*, I thought. Not to mention I had not yet reached my writing goal for the week. *Wait, did I even set the writing goal for this week?* I thought. *Ugh . . .*

None of these negative thoughts were catastrophic. Nothing I was dealing with was life-or-death. I wasn't in danger. But my thoughts snowballed until I lay down on the sofa and distracted myself with games, mindless scrolling, and a couple of phone calls with friends. I'm not saying those actions were bad—connecting with a friend is a good thing even if it is done out of procrastination—but they were not how I had hoped to spend the day.

Resilience isn't simply about the big setbacks and challenges. There are even more opportunities to use the rules of resilience for the mundane, everyday challenges that threaten to throw off your perfectly good days and turn them into real downers. If enough of those days stack up, you've got a bad habit. Habits are ultimately what create success or failure, happiness or misery.

It wasn't until about noon on Saturday that I realized that if my negative attitude extended through the weekend, it would lead only to regret and frustration come Monday. I knew I needed to seize the opportunity to practice resilience with this rule: "Choose thoughts that strengthen you."

It wasn't what was happening that was ruining my mood. It was what I was saying to myself about the things that were happening:

Something bad is going to happen.

Bad things have happened.

More bad things will happen if you don't get it together.

You have too much on your plate to take a break. And it's all your fault. You overcommitted and now you're stuck.

What's wrong with you? Why are you always a time optimist? Didn't you write a book about how to stop doing that? And now you are sitting here wasting time thinking about how you're wasting time!

Yeah, the back-to-back thoughts swirling in my head had me stuck and starting to feel defeated. Nothing awful had happened. But I was telling myself that everything was awful and getting worse and that it was all my fault. That is, until my awareness interrupted my thoughts. *That's anxiety*, I said to myself.

I was practicing a simple technique called "affect labeling," the act of naming the emotion I was feeling and observing.[1] By stopping to label it, I interrupted the rapid automatic thoughts that were occupying my mind. The break allowed me time to take a breath and notice what I was telling myself. They were not mindful thoughts, but mindless, unexamined, fear-based speculation that wasn't helpful but was actually getting me stuck.

I decided to come up with some new, helpful thoughts. I did so by coaching myself with some simple questions that could move me to resiliency in that moment. By being mindful of my thoughts and choosing them intentionally, I could coach myself to a different mindset. So I asked myself,

What would it look like to take responsibility for my thoughts right now?

How would it feel to take responsibility?

How do I want to feel?

What would I need to do to feel that way?

Just asking these questions almost immediately shifted how I felt. A tinge of hope flickered in my chest—kind of like that feeling you get when you're excited about something. It wasn't overwhelming, but it was palpable. And I liked it. As I leaned in to the questions, it was like a glimmer of the sun broke through the cloud that had been hovering over me. I thought through my answers one by one. They sounded something like this.

What would it look like to take responsibility for my thoughts right now? *Taking responsibility right now would look like making a plan to move forward, setting a clear goal, maybe leaving the house and going to the coffee shop down the street to write for a couple of hours. It would also look like noticing my blessings, rather than dwelling on the stuff that has me feeling down. Everything I am dealing with is real. It is also manageable. It's just life. I don't want to keep making it a big deal. The way forward is to keep moving forward, imperfectly.*

How would it feel to take responsibility? *Taking responsibility would feel good. It would give me confidence. It would make me feel happy and grateful. I can't blame anyone or anything when I take responsibility, so almost immediately, I stop feeling sorry for myself. On Friday, a part of me wanted to wallow in self-pity. And I let it have its way. But that gets old pretty quickly. I think I've had enough of it.*

How do I want to feel? *Good. I want to feel good. Capable. Happy. Relaxed. Purposeful. Helpful.*

What would I need to do to feel that way? *I'd have to think different thoughts than I have been for the previous couple of days. And maybe have a little self-compassion. I expected to have a summer hiatus for the fourth summer in a row, but I wasn't realistic about projects and due dates. I hate to admit that I need to accept that reality and plan better next year. I'm disappointed that I was overly optimistic. It's hard. But it's not the end of the world. I need to adjust my expectations.*

When You Change What You Think

Keandra, a surgeon, is the married mother of three children. When she's at work, she feels guilty that she's not in the car line picking her kids up from school. When she's at home, she feels guilty that she's not doing the research she wants to be doing to advance her career. Keandra feels caught between a rock and a hard place! Whatever your circumstances, perhaps you can relate.

It's likely no surprise that women are far more likely to feel guilt—real guilt *and* false guilt!—than men. But if you're a woman, I want you to hear that you don't have to be bullied by those thoughts insisting that you're failing at everything. When you're able to notice that kind of thought and label it, you can interrupt it and take action based on it.

Keandra made the decision to do just that. Reading an article about the benefits children of working moms experience, Keandra learned that these children have more confidence. Boys are more likely to grow up to be men who become equal partners in relationships. And more. So as Keandra began to notice those thoughts, she made the choice to replace them with new thoughts that strengthened her.

"I am blessing my family financially."

"My work is a springboard to talk to my children about *their* purpose."

"I can help my children notice their own unique gifts and begin to dream."

Keandra found freedom when she chose to change the way she thought.

Perhaps the most immediately transformative rule of resilience is that when you change your thoughts, you change how you feel and what you do. So much of our life experience is not what actually happens to and around us, but *what we tell ourselves* about what is happening to and around us. If you can embrace this one truth, you can use it to transform your life. Psychology and faith both confirm it. As people think, so they are, Proverbs 23:7 tells us, promising that our thoughts become our reality.[2]

Our thoughts become our reality.

The power of what we tell ourselves became a central theme of psychology beginning in the mid-twentieth century. At that time, most psychiatrists subscribed to the Freudian theory of psychoanalysis. They believed that analyzing a person's past would explain their responses to current challenges. This theory asserts that people have unconscious and repressed memories, feelings, desires, and thoughts. Psychoanalysis should be used to identify those emotions and experiences, leading to catharsis and healing. This is the type of therapy we often associate with a patient lying on a sofa while a therapist asks them questions about their childhood.

As a young psychiatrist, Dr. Aaron T. Beck assumed Freud's theory was correct; however, he believed more research was needed to validate it. He expected that his research with patients battling depression would confirm the psychoanalytic understanding that this condition was the expression of anger turned inward by patients with an innate need to suffer.

However, Dr. Beck's research refuted these assumptions. He noticed that patients, when discussing themselves and their situations, often shared spontaneous negative beliefs, which he termed "automatic thoughts."[3] He then observed that these thoughts—even more than the patients' situations—were what drove their responses to the challenges they faced. He worked with patients to change their thoughts and choose healthier behaviors in response to their situations. For example, he treated patients who used overeating or alcohol as dysfunctional attempts to cope with stress and sadness.

Further research into Dr. Beck's approach showed that it changed how patients felt about their circumstances. Eventually his findings led Dr. Beck to develop cognitive theory, which over time became known as cognitive behavioral therapy (CBT). *Cognitive* simply refers to what you know, learn, and understand; in other words, what you think. The cognitive-behavioral process connects your thoughts and your behavior. Practically speaking, you can decide whether or not your thoughts are helpful and then decide whether to keep thinking them.

By the 1970s, clinical trials validating the effectiveness of cognitive behavioral therapy catapulted the theory into practice internationally. Today, Beck, who served as a professor of psychiatry at the University of Pennsylvania for nearly seventy years, is viewed as the pioneer in advancing the practical benefits of learning to change self-defeating thoughts.[4]

Thought Awareness: Learning to Think on Purpose

Most people don't pay much attention to their thoughts. And even if they do notice them, they may not realize that they don't have to simply accept whatever thoughts show up. At the core of resilience is the ability to examine your thoughts, decide whether they are helpful, and intentionally choose thoughts that strengthen rather than weaken you. Focusing on changing the way we think is an example of an adaptive skill.

Let's take a look at a powerful framework and tool for resilience. I invite you to commit this to memory and practice it until it becomes your habit. The first part of this structure is a skill to build your thought awareness. I'll then expand the stressor-thought-reaction (STR) framework to show you how to connect your thoughts to your vision and actions so you can make powerful shifts that transform your ability to persevere and thrive in the face of challenges and adversity.

THOUGHT AWARENESS

Stressor → Thoughts → Reactions

We tend to think that we go directly from the stressor that triggers us to the reaction we have to the challenge. So, for example, a road rage incident may be explained by someone getting cut off in traffic, becoming angry, and then chasing the other driver down and starting an altercation. But many of us have been cut off in traffic and did not react by chasing the offender and starting a fight. What's the difference? Between the stressor (getting cut off in traffic) and the reaction (angrily chasing someone down and starting an altercation), there was a thought.

When I get cut off in traffic, I may be annoyed for a moment, but I don't tell myself, *No one cuts me off. That's disrespectful. I'm going to make them pay!* My thoughts are more like, *That was rude! Well, maybe they're just a jerk or maybe they're in a hurry to get to an emergency.* I then take a breath, slow down, and let them go on. The thought *Maybe they're just a jerk* irritates me, but I accept that there are a lot of inconsiderate people in the world and do my best not to engage with them. Such people are a nuisance, and at times even dangerous, so I want to limit my interactions with them. The thought *Maybe they are in a hurry to get to an emergency* leaves me feeling empathetic, not vengeful. It may be entirely untrue, but it doesn't matter. In the long run, it serves me well and keeps me safe.

The point is, two people can have a similar stressor and a completely different reaction because their thoughts about the stressor differ. The exciting element of this is that even though we don't control the thoughts that show up, we can decide whether those thoughts serve us well. If they don't, we can choose new ones.

Such thought awareness is especially important when you are reacting to circumstances in a way that is counterproductive to the outcome you desire.

Now let's use the skill of thought awareness and the STR framework to evaluate a recent event.[5] Consider a recent vivid, specific situation in which you had a counterproductive reaction. Perhaps you lost your temper with a rude customer service rep, you flubbed a presentation because your confidence waned, or you procrastinated and missed a deadline. It could be any situation, but choose something specific and recent.

Begin by noting the stressor and your reaction—the two elements that are easier to name.

Stressor: What happened? Detail only what happened, not your interpretations and opinions about what happened. Identify the stressor in a neutral way, listing who, what, when, and where it occurred, but not *why* it occurred. Leave out the why because that is your interpretation of the event. Therefore, it is a thought about the stressor, not the stressor itself.

Reaction: How did you respond? Next, identify what you felt, said, or did when faced with this stressor. Reactions are your emotions and actions.

Next take some time to consider what comes in between—how your interpretation of the stressor led to your reaction.

Thought: Why did it happen? Your interpretation is your explanation of why something happened. An interpretation is an opinion, filtered by your previous experiences and influences, as well as your current fears, hopes, or other factors. In essence, it's your thought(s) about what happened, and those thoughts create your reaction. By neutrally describing the stressor, you remove the emotion- and opinion-infused descriptions. The same stressor leads to different reactions *because* of your interpretation of it.

How Did You Interpret That?

Resilience isn't tested until you face a stressor. How you react to that challenge determines how resilient you are *in the moment*. I say "in the moment" because resilience is not a fixed outcome. It changes over time. Sometimes it even looks messy, as though you aren't resilient at all. "Fall seven times, but stand up eight" is a Japanese saying that sums up a healthy view of resilience.

When it comes to thought awareness, the key is noticing how you interpret adverse events when they occur. It's not what happens that matters most; it's what you say to yourself about what happens that matters most. Your thoughts about the events of your life are more powerful than the events themselves. Why? Because it is your thoughts that create your reactions (emotions and actions). It is your interpretation of events that you must be intentional about if you are to be resilient.

So if the key to changing your reactions is changing your thoughts, how do you go about doing that? For example, if you've prepared for a performance—whether a sales presentation, an athletic event, or an intimidating conversation—but feel doubtful and anxious beforehand, thought awareness will likely reveal thoughts that line up with what you are feeling. *I don't know if I can do this*, *This isn't going to go well*, or *The odds are stacked against me* are a few of the thoughts that could sap your confidence. If you take a breath and consciously become aware of those thoughts, you can intentionally focus on a new thought. Two questions can coach you to the right new thought:

- What do you want to feel instead of doubtful or anxious?
- Whatever your answer to the above question, what thought would lead to that feeling?

Perhaps your answer to that first question would be "I want to feel confident and strong." Your answer to the second question would perhaps be, "I am ready. I am prepared. I've got this." Sometimes we simply need to remind ourselves of what we already know and what is already true.

THOUGHT INVENTORY

Take a moment to consider a challenge you are currently struggling to conquer and how you feel about it. Call to mind the actions, or lack thereof, that are counterproductive to succeeding in the face of this challenge. Creating a thought inventory is the first step to noticing what you're saying to yourself and how you're interpreting the present circumstances.

Identify the current challenge that has you stuck:

What are you saying to yourself about the challenge? Make a list here. This is your thought inventory for that challenge.

1. ______________________________
____

2. ______________________________
____

3. ______________________________
____

4. ______________________________
____

5. ______________________________
____

THOUGHT REPLACEMENTS

Ask yourself whether each thought is helpful or counterproductive—or whether it moves you forward or keeps you stuck. A counterproductive thought is one that holds you back from the goal or outcome you desire. For each counterproductive thought, identify a new, productive thought to replace it. For example, the thought *I don't know if I can do this* can be replaced with *I've got this.* The thought *I don't deserve more* can be replaced with *I deserve good things in my life.* The thought *This mistake will ruin my career* can be replaced with *I am determined to learn from this mistake, and I will not give up.*

The best time to identify thought replacements is when you are in a positive frame of mind. The most resilient people have these thoughts ready so they can replace their most persistent counterproductive thoughts. Remember, positive emotions broaden your scope of thinking and make it easier for you to see new and better thoughts. This doesn't mean you cannot do it in the heat of the moment when you are having a counterproductive thought—you can. But it is easier to do it when your mind is calm and confident.

Take a moment to consider some replacement thoughts for the thought inventory you just did. Start with the most persistent, counterproductive thought on your list. Then counter each of those thoughts with one that would lead to an emotion or action you actually want to have.

1. ______________________________
____

2. ______________________________
____

3. ______________________________
____

4. ______________________________
____

5. ______________________________
____

WHAT WOULD BE A MORE USEFUL INTERPRETATION?

The good news about thoughts is that we can change them. Your interpretation of events is critical to your resilience. By interpretation, I mean the story you tell yourself that answers these questions:

- What happened?
- What is happening now?
- What will happen in the future?
- Why has any of it happened—now, in the past, or in the future?

Your answers to these questions reveal your thoughts. Those thoughts create your reactions—what you feel, say, and do. Therefore, your ability to practice thought awareness—making the connection between your thoughts and the emotions and actions they lead to—is pivotal. When you recognize that your interpretation of events is counterproductive, your job is to search for a more useful interpretation. This takes practice. The better you get at interpreting the events and circumstances that come your way, the more resilient you become.

No one gets this right all the time. A part of being human is becoming discouraged at times. Doubts creep in. Fear is natural. Discouragement is inevitable sometimes. But ask yourself, *What am I saying to myself that leaves me feeling this way? What might be a more useful interpretation?* Take a breath and answer wholeheartedly.

WHAT DO YOU DO WHEN YOUR INTERPRETATION IS NEGATIVE AND ACCURATE?

Sometimes the thought you have is negative and unhelpful—but actually true. Maybe you did make a huge mistake. You bombed the project. Failed the test. Damaged the relationship. Maybe it is all your fault. In such instances, replacing the thought *I failed at this, and I am such a failure* with *I was great! I don't know why the client can't see how good we are!* would be untruthful and inauthentic, and therefore, counterproductive. What do you do then?

When the truth is both negative and accurate, you must ask, *In light of the reality, how do I want to show up in this situation?* When you shift your focus in this way, you have the opportunity to work on personal growth or character development. This is where Resilience Rule #2, "Choose thoughts that strengthen you," converges with Resilience Rule #7: "Don't pretend, don't defend." By acknowledging the unwanted truth, you muster the courage to face it. You can conquer what you are willing to confront. Your

You can conquer what you are willing to confront.

thought replacement should acknowledge the truth while landing on a replacement thought that reflects how you want to show up in a way that will help you face the problem in the future.

For example, you might replace the thought *I failed at this because I'm a massive failure!* with *I failed at this because I have some learning to do, and I am putting steps in place to get started next week to learn so I can succeed on this project next time.*

Speak Life in the Face of Death

International track champion Chaunté Lowe did what most athletes only dream of—competing in four summer Olympic games. There's a very good chance she would have made a fifth consecutive Olympic appearance if not for a serious health diagnosis in 2019. One day that year, she noticed a tiny knot in her breast tissue. Not long afterward, she was diagnosed with triple-negative breast cancer, which is one of the most aggressive forms.[6] Her first reaction was tremendous fear that her life might be ending. She says it wasn't her life that flashed before her eyes, but the lives of her children. She recalls standing in her closet, crushed, and telling her husband she was sorry she would be leaving him to raise their kids alone.

Her husband, who is also a competitive track athlete and triple jumper, refused to go down that line of thinking. "You have been a fighter your entire life," he reminded her. "Now is the time to fight!" Her husband's simple but powerful words resonated and shifted her entire perspective.

"I was devastated for about ten minutes," she recalls. "And then I realized, he is right! It's time to fight. I started talking to myself. In my head, I said, *You got this.*" We have the power to speak life or death into a situation, she says. "I had a goal, and that goal was to live. And what I said about my situation in my mind was going to make the difference between me living or dying.

"On some days," she admits, "the thoughts were overwhelming, and it was hard to stay focused and maintain hope."

So on a good day when she felt hopeful, she decided to record herself talking to herself. That way, on especially difficult days following her double mastectomy and then rounds of chemotherapy, she could remind herself to fight and maintain her hope. On those days when she didn't feel like persevering in the fight, she would play the recording to redirect her thoughts:

> Chaunté, you have to remember to keep going, keep pushing, keep pushing. Even if you have to go outside and walk or jog, every little step is going to count toward your goal. Chaunté, get up out of the bed! I understand sometimes you're going to need to rest, but if you can get out of the bed, get up! You have a lot to live for. Chaunté, you can do it! Get up out of the bed! Go play with your kids. Get up!

Chaunté let those words inspire her. Today she's cancer-free and speaks to audiences around the world about pushing through challenges by choosing thoughts that strengthen, focus, and prepare you to surmount major obstacles. While the obstacles we face are not always a matter of life or death like Chaunté's cancer diagnosis, the principle remains the same. In fact, there is a practice you can embrace that combines the power of vision and the STR (stressor, thoughts, reactions) process to achieve any goal.

Vision → STR → Result

STEP 1: VISION

Start with your vision, specifically the goal within your vision that you want to achieve right now. A vision can be made up of many goals, so choose one goal for this process. This will enable you to be specific in pinpointing obstacles to it.

Even though you may be going through a difficulty, you start with vision, which answers the coaching question: What do you want? This enables you to focus on the vision rather than the obstacle. Chaunté's goal was to live! Your goal could be a promotion in the next year or retirement at a certain age or recovering fully from a financial setback or relationship problem. Describe exactly what it is that you want to see happen.

STEP 2: IDENTIFY THE STRESSOR THAT THREATENS TO DERAIL YOUR GOAL

Identify the obstacle that is most likely to keep you from getting to the goal. In Chaunté's case, it was the cancer that had a high mortality rate. If your goal is a promotion, the obstacle could be competition among your peer group. If the goal is recovery from a financial setback, the obstacle could be lack of enough income to pay off debt.

STEP 3: IDENTIFY COUNTERPRODUCTIVE THOUGHT INTERPRETATIONS AND REPLACE THEM WITH PRODUCTIVE ONES

Articulate the thoughts you're having about the stressor and how they may be causing reactions that are counter to your goal. For example, Chaunté's thought, *I'm not going to be here to see my kids grow up* was demotivating, leading to the reaction of staying in bed rather than getting up and moving, which would help her recovery. If your goal is a promotion and you face stiff competition, the thought *I'm not as capable so I might as well stop trying* might lead to the reaction of giving up on the goal. Once you become aware of that thought, however, you can choose to see the need for a new thought, such as *If I shore up my skills, I could make a more impactful contribution to the team and maybe even surpass my competition.* That thought could motivate you to be honest about where and how you need to grow, leading you to develop skills that will increase your chances for a promotion.

STEP 4: FOLLOW THROUGH ON REACTIONS THAT MOVE YOU TOWARD THE GOAL

Notice how your reactions—what you feel, say, and do—are moving you in the right direction, and notice the thoughts that are empowering those reactions. Practice thinking productive thoughts until they become automatic, creating consistent, positive action toward your goal.

STEP 5: GET THE RESULT YOU ENVISIONED IN STEP 1

When you are resilient through each of these steps, you will see results. This process takes practice, but it works!

Mindfulness

Mindfulness is simply paying attention on purpose. When it comes to your thoughts, mindfulness can be the key that opens the door to changing how you feel and what you do—your reactions to the things that happen in your life.

Sandra used mindfulness to stop herself from going down a negative spiral recently. An accountant who runs her own small firm, she had been told the week before by a remote team member that he was leaving to take another job. She felt conflicted. On the one hand, Chad wasn't always a reliable performer. Without notifying her in advance, he sometimes took time off and handled personal matters during work hours.

On the other hand, it was during her busy season, so the timing wasn't the best. Even so, she understood and knew that Chad had been given a great opportunity. She also appreciated that he had the courtesy to give her two weeks' notice. At the end of the first week, Sandra finalized the plan for his final week to ensure a smooth transition. Then when she arrived at the office the following Monday morning, Maria, a senior team member, mentioned that Chad was already onboarding for his new job. Sandra was blindsided. She had expected to use this week to tie up loose ends to be sure nothing fell through the cracks when he left.

When Sandra went back to her office and checked her email, she saw that Chad had sent her a similar message. He told her that the new employer asked him to move up his start date by a week. He would still try to get some things done for Sandra that week, but he wouldn't be fully available. The tone of the email rubbed her the wrong way, and it reminded her of other times when he hadn't communicated well.

A flurry of automatic thoughts flooded Sandra's mind, and each negative thought agitated her more than the previous one. It was a downward spiral.

We are paying him to work this week and he's working somewhere else!

As a business owner, I try so hard to treat people well, but I can't expect the same in return. It seems everyone is just out for themselves these days!

No one cares about keeping their word or not burning bridges!

I'm so sick of managing people! This just confirms what I've been thinking—I need to sell this business and retire!

Sandra had started the day feeling energized by the transition plan she'd created with Chad the previous week, and now it had been upended. In a matter of seconds, she could feel her whole body tense up. Her breathing was shallow, her shoulders tight, and her lips pursed as she rose hurriedly from her desk and walked to the window. She gazed out as the soft drizzle that had persisted all morning turned to full raindrops. She placed her hand on her forehead and let out a loud sigh as she pondered the flurry of frustrated thoughts. In the distance, she could see a glimmer of sunlight breaking through the clouds. It was a sign, perhaps, and an invitation to take a breath and pause.

Sandra and I had been coaching for nearly a year by this point, and the theme of our coaching revolved around building resilience to navigate the challenges and opportunities she faced running a successful business. She remembered this as she paused.

Do I like how I am feeling right now? she asked herself, aware that she was spiraling downward in a puddle of stress and anxiety.

No, was the clear answer.

Her flurry of automatic thoughts were honest. They were the default thoughts that emerged upon being blindsided by the news that Chad's last full day had actually been the previous week, and there was nothing she could do about it. She decided in that moment to redirect her thoughts. The reason? She did not want to feel stressed. She did not want to feel angry. And she did not want to waste time and energy rehashing something she could not change. She needed to focus forward. So she chose a new set of thoughts.

You did a good job last week working with Chad to prepare for the transition.

Chad has already done quite a bit to get things in order for his replacement.

You have a team, and everyone will rally together to move forward positively if you remain positive.

You have the power to choose your response to this email in a way that is authentic and works in the best interest of your vision and state of mind.

After that last thought, Sandra replied to Chad's email very simply: "What will be your work hours this week?" She recognized that she could not control how Chad chose to leave the company. Her broad thought about how no one keeps their word anymore left her feeling angry, powerless, and stressed. These thoughts weakened her and did not help her focus on getting through the challenge resiliently. Unless she chose thoughts that strengthened her, she would waste the time Chad had left in his position and possibly create animosity between them that would sabotage her ultimate goal—ensuring a smooth transition and gathering all the information needed before Chad left. She decided to control the controllable—working within the hours Chad had available. She laser-focused on her most important goal—minimizing the disruption to business caused by his turnover. These new thoughts caused her to ask him some proactive questions. "What will be your work hours this week?" was the first question she needed in order to formulate the game plan.

Chad responded immediately with specific times and clarified how he planned to finish the tasks at her office.

Sandra reflected on the situation in a coaching session. "I could feel myself getting worked up," she recalled. "When Maria mentioned that Chad was transitioning a week early, the negative thoughts rushed in so fast. It was instant. I was upset. Immediately, I verbalized what I was thinking. And Maria kind of just echoed what I was saying. She understood.

"When I went back to my office, I was irritated and deflated. In a matter of minutes, my automatic thoughts had hijacked the motivation and energy I'd started my day with. As I stood at the window, it occurred to me that my thoughts were not helping me. They were draining my energy and paralyzing me with negative emotions."

Sandra's initial response was normal. What she did in that moment is what we all need to do when we are thrown off track. We can be mindful about what we are saying to ourselves. We don't necessarily control the thoughts that show up. But if we notice them rather than allow them to take over our entire thought process, we can decide whether the thoughts are worth keeping or if they need to be replaced.

How to Take Your Thoughts Off Autopilot

When do you find yourself having automatic thoughts that derail your energy or get you stuck?

The most resilient people say something different to themselves in the face of their challenges. Their thinking is not on autopilot. When their thoughts create reactions that are counterproductive to the outcome they want, they notice those thoughts and consciously change them. This takes practice and intention. Neuroscience shows that long-held thought habits, especially the kind that create fear, become an embedded pattern in our brains.

Dr. Ebony Glover had recently completed a PhD in neuroscience at Emory University when she joined the first cohort of graduates from The CaPP Institute's Coach Training Intensive in 2010. I was fascinated by her studies and curious about what neuroscience might say about resilience and the power of coaching. Now an associate professor of neuroscience at Kennesaw State University, Dr. Glover conducts research designed to better understand biological and environmental factors associated with fear and anxiety behaviors as a means of helping reduce mental health disparities. It's a fascinating field of study. When your experiences create thoughts and emotions such as fear and anxiety, the impact is serious.

"Fear is, at its root, a biological construct," Dr. Glover told me when I interviewed her about resilience and neuroscience on the *Coaching and Positive Psychology* podcast. "It's a physical thing and not just some phantom emotion. It actually exists in the form of molecules, amino acids, proteins, cells, and chemicals in the body. While fear is often triggered by events outside of you—events in the world—it actually lives in your brain."[7]

The repeated STR (stressor-thought-reaction) process creates patterns in the brain similar to the way water digs grooves in the earth. Soon the grooves get deeper and wider and become streams. Water flows naturally toward them. Your thoughts are similar. You get into a pattern. When a stressor appears, your thought pattern can be automatic. And in order to create a new pattern, you'll need to intentionally think something new, one thought at a time, digging a new groove and slowly drying up the old pattern of thoughts.

Don't be discouraged if it's hard at first, or if you choose thoughts that strengthen you one day, only to fall victim to counterproductive thoughts and feel like giving up the next. This is normal. I've been teaching this framework for years, and I'm still practicing! But as you keep replacing counterproductive thought interpretations with helpful thoughts, your new interpretations will become your norm. Practice is like building muscle. With repetition, you'll get stronger over time.

Coach Yourself

- What's the goal or outcome you want to practice the STR framework with?
- What's a stressor (fear/habit/distraction) that gets in your way?
- What thoughts do you have when this stressor appears?
- What reaction (in the form of feelings, words, or actions) occurs as a result of the thought?

- What happens as a result of that reaction?

Now, let's go back to the top and reframe this situation. Your answers to the first two questions above will be the same as before, but let's replace the others with a new set of questions so you can choose some new thoughts.

- What mindful thought might you choose when your stressor appears?
- What reaction would that mindful thought create?
- What will be the outcome when you react to the mindful thought in that way?
- When will you apply this in your situation?
- In what other situation(s) do you need to walk through this process?
- When will you do that?

Try This

- ☐ Identify a goal you have that feels challenging because you keep getting stuck.
- ☐ Complete a thought inventory by making a list of all the thoughts you have about this goal, especially the counterproductive and unhelpful ones.
- ☐ Use the Coach Yourself questions above to walk through each stage of the five-step Vision-STR-Result framework.

SAY IT WITH ME:

"When I change my thoughts, I change how I feel and what I do."

RESILIENCE RULE #3

FOCUS ON THE VISION, NOT THE OBSTACLE

How a personal vision manifesto will pull you forward, especially when you get stuck

---

KEY MESSAGES

- Focus on the vision; work around the obstacle.
- Create your Vision Manifesto and use it as a tool to get unstuck.
- Knowing the five stages of success will enhance your patience, endurance, and results.

At twenty-five, I had the audacious idea that I wanted a book deal with a major publisher. It's a dream many people have—and at least as many people will tell you all the reasons it's a dream unlikely to be fulfilled. Considering that 99 percent of book proposals are rejected by traditional publishing houses, statistically they are correct.[1]

There are few career fields with such a dismal chance of success. Yet it felt deeply purposeful for me. I can remember the first time the thought of becoming an author crossed my mind. During my first semester of graduate school in journalism, I had a flash of inspiration—*I want to write books!* Doing so would allow me to have a career and a family. Somehow, even at the age of twenty, I knew I wanted freedom and flexibility. Back then, it was just a vision without a clear purpose behind it. The obstacles were many—becoming a good enough writer, having something worthwhile to write about, and of course, figuring out how to beat the odds and get published, let alone earning a living at it. My first attempt at writing a book came just two years later. My enthusiasm was there, but the content was not. After about ten thousand words, I had absolutely nothing left to say. That might be the only time in my life that I've run out of words!

Three more years passed before I tried again. This time, I studied a book on publishing first.[2] I followed the instructions about how to write a query letter to pitch to literary agents. My core fear is rejection, but I mustered the nerve to reach out to six agents about my book idea. Two said no, three never wrote back, and one said yes! I'd researched the agents' interests, and it turned out that the agent who agreed to represent me spoke some German and loved airplanes. I lived in Germany as a kid and once wanted to be a pilot—two facts I wove into my query letter.

With my agent's connections, we caught the interest of a Random House imprint. I couldn't believe my good fortune! They asked for a sample chapter, which I nervously wrote. I thought it was good. Unfortunately, they decided to pass. *Ouch.* I was disappointed but also encouraged. At least I'd gotten their attention.

Soon my agent landed a book deal for me with a small publisher. Within a few months, though, the publisher ran into financial trouble and the whole deal fell through. Once again, I was disappointed. My agent moved on to other projects, and I focused on my day job running my PR firm.

While I had not yet achieved my vision of becoming an author, I saw these obstacles as opportunities for growth. The Random House editor who rejected my book had been kind enough to give specific feedback about my writing. They had wanted more stories and more of my voice to shine through. Upon reflecting on the feedback, I realized I had been writing for the publisher's approval rather than from a place of passion and purpose. That made me ask myself, *What is my purpose? Besides wanting a career that would give me flexibility and freedom while using my writing gift, what is my purpose for writing a book at all?*

Clarity didn't come until the following year when I had an epiphany: My purpose is inspiring others to live more fulfilling lives, using writing and speaking as the vehicle to do it. I'd tried to write a book three times in the previous four years. Now that I knew my purpose, could my fourth attempt make it into print?

I was still intimidated by the odds, but the possibility of success kindled a spark of hope. And that hope ignited a flame of curiosity. *How can I get a solid book deal? What do I have to do to make that a real possibility?* Curiosity was the key that unlocked pivotal questions whose answers revealed a winning plan for me. It was an example of an important rule of resilience: "Focus on the vision, not the obstacle."

When you're faced with an obstacle, this one rule can shift your perspective and inspire the kind of dogged perseverance and strategic approach—the resilience—that can get you to your goal. To be clear, I'm not suggesting that you ignore your obstacle. Quite the opposite. You see the obstacle clearly. You might even be intimidated by it, but you refuse to be overwhelmed to the point of giving up on your vision. Remember, it's not just positive thinking but accurate thinking about your challenges that helps you create a game plan to overcome them. My first book-writing attempt petered out because I ran out of words; the second attempt ended because a major publisher's interest in my writing fizzled; and the third fell through because a smaller publisher ran out of money. Even so, I couldn't let go of the vision of getting published by a major publisher. Have a vision that is so compelling that it's like a magnet that pulls you forward, even when obstacles threaten to discourage you.

What Do Successful People Do Differently?

Once I decided I wanted to land a book deal, my focus wasn't on the 99 percent of aspiring authors who never sign with a publisher. That fact pointed to the biggest obstacle to my vision: Lots of writers want a book deal, but there are a limited number of book deals being offered. Instead of focusing on the obstacle, though, I became intensely curious about one question: *What are the one percent of people doing differently?* They must have something—or a set of somethings—in common. *What is their secret sauce?* This is what I longed to discover. I didn't know any authors with book deals. So how could I learn what they do? Was there a manual? Was there a way to meet and talk to a successful author?

I started discussing my goal in personal and professional circles. I lived in Dallas at the time, and multiple sources led me to two names—local authors who had self-published fiction and then landed deals with major publishers. Until then, I had not considered self-publishing.

When I found out that the two local authors had hired the same local graphic designer to create their book covers, I hired him to design my cover too. I asked him if he'd see if these writers would be willing to chat with me. Both were. After meeting with them, I followed their advice. I also read everything I could find about how to write, market, and publish a book. With that knowledge, I made a game plan. Writing and self-publishing a book would be a big undertaking and commitment, especially while I ran another business full-time.

I had debt from credit card, auto, and student loans, not to mention my mortgage. But I felt the lack of money was a surmountable problem if I didn't lose sight of the vision—self-publishing and then a book deal. My plan was to use one of my credit cards to borrow $6,000 to print three thousand books—while being mindful of the ramifications if I didn't recoup the investment in book sales! I calculated that I would have to sell a little more than four hundred copies at the $14.95 price point to break even. My plan worked. With *Rich Minds, Rich Rewards* hot off the presses of a local printer the day before Thanksgiving 1999, I sold four hundred copies in the first three weeks, promising to autograph them for those who wanted to use them as Christmas gifts.

I was the author, editor, publisher, publicist, sales force, customer service rep, bookkeeper, and distributor. Within three months, the self-published book had been picked up by Barnes & Noble, which opened the door for a distributor to carry it and more stores to place orders. I pitched the book to local media, which resulted in interviews on local TV and radio stations. *The Dallas Morning News* ran a full feature story on the front of their lifestyle section. I walked into independent bookstores in Dallas and asked if they'd carry the book on consignment. Every one of them did. One bookseller invited me to give away books at a book reception she was helping to plan at BookExpo America in Chicago the following summer. I flew myself there and lugged two hundred copies of my book to the reception. As I was signing copies, a young woman came through the line. As it turns out, she headed up a brand-new Random House imprint aimed at reaching the newly sought-after African American reading audience with fiction. Even though my nonfiction book was designed to benefit everyone, she read the book on her plane ride back to New York and called the following Monday to offer me a book deal![3]

If at any point in my yearslong journey I'd focused on the extremely low odds of a first-time author landing a book deal, I would not have even wasted my time trying. The only way I knew to have enough hope to go after my dream was to focus on what the successful authors did differently from everyone else.

Succeeding in Spite of the Obstacles

As a young, bright-eyed twenty-two-year-old straight out of journalism school, I worked in the marketing department of an accounting firm. At that time, out of the company's one hundred–plus employees, there was one other black person, who quickly informed me that there had never been a black person in management in the forty-five-year history of the company.

But when the director of marketing was fired, I thought, *I could do this job.* Was I just twenty-two years old? Well, sure. Had I held a full-time job for just three months? Also, yes. I wasn't interested in focusing on the obstacles. Instead, I set my mind on the vision. I gave them the benefit of the doubt that they might give me a shot, and they did. I was promoted to marketing director.

Later in this chapter, I will coach you on how to define your own vision and the steps you'll need to get there. Many people, even before they outline their purpose and goals, sabotage their future success by noticing everything that might get in their way. With that in mind, I challenge you to consider this question: What do people who overcome their obstacles have in common? Rather than allowing the obstacle to overwhelm them, they stay focused on the vision—not only the purpose that fuels it, but also the key actions, habits, and attitude needed to reach their goal.

The most resilient people have an optimistic thinking style. That means they don't just think positively, they think accurately. They are not Pollyanna thinkers who cannot see just how hard a situation is. They see reality. They research options and plan accordingly while being realistic about the resources, timeline, and energy required to meet their goal. They see the potential problems clearly while also believing they can find a way to work around or through them. They expect the journey to be challenging, so they are less surprised and frustrated by challenges.

Research on goal-setting theory says that the bigger the goal, the bigger your commitment to reach it must be.[4] If the odds for success are low—whether a vocational, financial, relational, or physical goal—don't focus on how unlikely it is. Instead, work on getting clarity about what it will take to reach it. Look soberly at the barrier and take seriously the need for a realistic game plan to overcome it. If you focus too much on the difficulty, it will begin to feel insurmountable. If you focus on the vision, you will keep the obstacle in perspective.

What makes this approach most powerful is not simply that you expect challenges, but that you make sure they do not become your focus. The power of this rule lies in taking your eyes off the obstacle and remembering what it will feel and look like to reach your vision on the other side.

Dark Times Can Make the Light Shine Brighter

There's something about our darkest times that can make the light more obvious. Even the tiniest of lights looks bright when it's pitch-black in the room. A strong vision is like that light when obstacles do their best to extinguish it. If you keep the vision in your line of sight, the obstacle can never fully block it.

When I met my friend Tara-Leigh Cobble at a retreat on Lake Austin in 2017, I didn't know she was just three months out of open-heart surgery. But I knew almost from the instant I met her that she had a deep inner strength. She was comfortable in her own skin and clear about her life's mission. Her voice and smile were full of warmth and friendliness, which made me feel instantly at ease.

"I had a burn in my back the size of a grapefruit," she remembers about that retreat where we met in 2017. "It was an electrocautery burn from open heart surgery. It was an open wound in my back for about four months, and that was from my second heart surgery in a span of two months." She hadn't just been dealing with physical adversity. She had been a full-time musician until this point, but the electrocautery also damaged her lungs, so she no longer had the lung capacity to be a vocalist.

"I was going through this job transition," she recalls, "and my sister had just passed away from brain cancer. So it was a time when the winds were blowing hard in what felt like every direction in my life."

She says when she thinks of resilience, two things come to mind: "Sometimes when we think of something that's strong, we think of something that is just unyielding. But when I was a kid, I had a family member who loved country music, and one of the songs she played over and over was a Tanya Tucker song that described a tree in a backyard that the wind can't knock down: 'The reason it's still standing / It was strong enough to bend.'[5]

"And to me that is like the picture of resilience," Tara-Leigh explains. "The way that you stay standing is you've got firm, deep roots, but you can adapt. Strength and adaptability are those two components that keep you from crumbling."

Tara-Leigh had many reasons to crumble—the simultaneous loss of her sister, her career, and her health. But she didn't. She attributes her resilience to her unwavering faith and the vision that emerged from it. Perhaps it's that combination of traits that helped propel her vision for a 365-episode, eight-minute daily podcast to help people read through the Bible chronologically in a year.

With all she's been through, I asked her which example of resilience in her life she is most proud of. Her response: *The Bible Recap*. As she describes it, when she started she had no idea what she was in for or what a monumental project it would turn into and the obstacles she'd have to overcome. The idea for the podcast came to her in prayer. When she started planning, she set aside thirteen months in which to create the twelve-month podcast. Before it launched, Tara-Leigh spent about one hundred hours a month preparing for the podcast, recording the first few episodes in December 2018. When the podcast launched on New Year's Day 2019, she hoped to attract three hundred listeners a week. At the time, she was leading a Bible study of about 1,200 people around the world and aimed to get about one-fourth of them to join her on this journey by reading and listening to the podcast. By the time she woke up at 10 a.m. that first day, she found over three hundred emails in her inbox from listeners. She was blown away. To say *The Bible Recap* was a hit is an understatement. By February, the podcast had garnered a whopping one million downloads, and by spring, *Forbes* magazine included it on its list of the top fifty podcasts in the United States. As of this writing, *The Bible Recap* has exceeded 400 million downloads and counting.

Tara-Leigh's relentless commitment to her vision gave her a focus that allowed purpose to fuel her perseverance. The unexpected happened as it took off, but she was ready to handle it—even though "handling it" took more time and energy than she'd ever imagined when she started. Obstacles appeared, and she always put those challenges in perspective and focused on the vision.

"I had read through the Bible ten times, and I had a stack of notebooks over a foot and a half tall that were full of notes I had taken in my years through the Bible. And so I thought, *Well, yeah, I know this book, and I can do this, and it'll take me about an hour a day.* I was very, very wrong! It took over my life." By mid-January 2019, publishers began emailing Tara-Leigh, asking her to turn the podcast into a book. But she was still busy trying to get the podcast written, sometimes completing episodes just a day and a half before they were uploaded.

Tara-Leigh's vision for her podcast was clear and compelling. She knew exactly what she wanted to do. In fact, this is how her marketing copy describes her podcast and the audience she aimed to serve:

> If you've ever closed your Bible and thought, "What did I just read?," this podcast is for you! In about 8 minutes a day, we'll give you a summary and highlight reel of that day's Bible reading from our 1-year chronological plan (free on the Bible app), and you can start anytime—it's always a good time to read the Bible![6]

Before she even started, Tara-Leigh had a vision of who she was talking to (people who wanted to read the Bible), why she was talking to them (they found Scripture confusing or impersonal), what their pain point was (they didn't have a lot of time), and what they were looking for (they wanted it to be easy, casual, and enjoyable so they could actually love reading the Bible). Because her vision was so specific, her action plan was clear-cut.

When Your Vision Is Clear, Prepare to Be Delighted

One thing Tara-Leigh didn't include in her vision, though, was a goal of reaching millions of people. "I dream small," she says with a laugh. "I am very easily pleased." With a vision so clear, executed with such passion, energy, and consistency, the podcast took off in ways she never even hoped for or imagined.

We don't necessarily control the end result of our vision, but we can be intentional about making sure the vision is clear. That part is controllable. Tara-Leigh's vision had a clear purpose: Make reading the Bible easy, consistent, and enjoyable. The purpose was the why, and the vision was the how. How did she do it? Bite-size, casual podcasts every single day covering about two pages at a time.

She focused relentlessly on the vision, and neither obstacles nor even the unexpected opportunities that arose because of her success could eclipse it. In fact, multiple publishers offered to publish a book of the same name before she had even completed the 365-day podcast. But once she'd made it through that first year, she was ready to tackle this new project and started on the book in early 2020. When the pandemic hit, she was isolated in her apartment, limited by health challenges that would have put her at dangerous risk if she contracted the virus. In retrospect, the lockdown may have seemed like an obstacle to other entrepreneurs, but she chose to reframe it as an opportunity that gave her a more intense focus and the quiet time she needed to study and pray.

A compelling vision is like a magnet that pulls you forward through the most stubborn obstacles.

In its first few years, *The Bible Recap* book sold more than a half million copies. Now Tara-Leigh is at work on a massive publishing deal spanning the next decade. The books also aim at making the stories and wisdom of Scripture more accessible, understandable, and enjoyable for adults. She is even working on a series for children. Tara-Leigh's dream was small, but her vision was sharp.

A compelling vision is like a magnet that pulls you forward through the most stubborn obstacles. Your vision is a vivid picture of what you want to see unfold at some given point in the future—whether the way your presentation is going to go next week or how you want your entire life to unfold ten years from now. Vision is critical to resilience because it pulls you forward when you might otherwise give up or get stuck.

Two Inspiring Tools: Your Vision Board and Vision Manifesto

I have found a couple of tools incredibly helpful when clarifying my own vision and helping others do the same.

VISION BOARD

A vision board is a collage of pictures and words that reflect your vision and inspire you to take action to bring it to life. You can create a digital vision board or a paper one—or both.

About ten years after my first book was published, I decided to create my first vision board. I filled a canvas with images representing my aspirations for achieving a happy marriage and motherhood; being invited onto NBC's *Today* show; traveling and enjoying Italy, France, and the South Florida beaches; and growing my business to seven figures, to name a few. One by one, the personal and professional goals on my vision board came to fruition. I connected with my husband, whom I'd gone to middle school and high school with in Colorado. He now lived in metro Atlanta, like me, and we married a little over a year later. I became a bonus mom and then mom. In 2013, I was invited onto *Today* for the first time and have since been invited back more than forty times. My business goal became my new normal, and now I've traveled to the places I'd dreamed of.

Large or small, your dreams may look very different from mine. Maybe you've had it in your heart to start a dessert catering business on the weekends. Perhaps you've set your mind on going back to school to earn a degree you've always wanted. Or you might want to fly on an airplane for the first time! Your goals are *your* goals. When you set your eyes on the prize, you may be surprised by the way your vision can help you overcome the obstacles in your path.

Your vision board can be simple to create. Here's the process I recommend and have seen work well for me, my clients, and members of my personal growth course, the Successful Women's Academy:

1. Identify the elements of the vision you'd like to see unfold.
2. Write a Vision Manifesto, a present-tense declaration of what you want your life to look like at a given point in the future.
3. Gather images that reflect your vision.

4. Arrange those images in a collage that you can place somewhere to be reminded daily of your vision. You might frame it and hang it on a wall, or digitize it and use it as background wallpaper on your computer or electronic devices.

VISION MANIFESTO

The first time I kicked off a Vision Board Challenge for my social media community, I challenged them to experiment with a second important exercise before creating a vision board. I call it a Vision Manifesto, and I had no idea just how powerful a step it would be in bringing people's visions to life. Within months, participants in the Vision Board Challenge began telling me about dream homes they'd bought and moved into, books they'd written, debt they'd paid off, health goals they'd achieved, and new jobs they'd landed. All of them credited their Vision Manifesto as the impetus to finally bring long-held dreams to life. It fascinated me because I've talked about vision for years, but something about writing about the vision before creating a visual of it seemed to give the board more power.

A Vision Manifesto is a present-tense declaration of what you want your life to look like in five key areas—relationships, work, finances, health, and spirituality. If you were to describe in the present tense how you want to live, work, and feel daily, what words would you use? The Vision Manifesto is a coaching tool I developed, inspired by the work of research psychologist Dr. Laura King, whose best possible future self exercise has been shown to have positive mental and physical benefits.

> The best possible selves (BPS) activity is a writing intervention . . . in which participants write about themselves in the future, imagining that everything has worked out in the best possible way. The instructions used for the BPS intervention are:

> Think about your life in the future. Imagine that everything has gone as well as it possibly could. You have worked hard and succeeded at accomplishing all of your life goals. Think of this as the realisation of all your life dreams. Now write about what you imagined.[7]

To create your own Vision Manifesto, coach yourself with the following questions:

- *Relationships.* In your vision, how do you think, act, and/or feel in your relationships? How do you impact others, and how are you impacted by them?
- *Work.* In your vision, how do you feel in your work? What values are reflected in your work? Where are you, what are you doing, and how is your life better because of it? What is the impact of the work you do on others?
- *Finances.* In your vision, how do you think, act, and/or feel about your finances? How do you handle your finances? What values are reflected in how you approach your finances? What does money enable you to do in your vision?
- *Health.* In your vision, how do you feel physically, and what is your attitude about your health? What do you do to sustain or improve your health? What does your health empower you to do?
- *Spiritual/mental/emotional.* In your vision, how do you show up mentally, emotionally, and/or spiritually? What do you do in the face of fears or difficulties? How do you think and act when opportunities arise? What principle always guides your approach to life?

Some in my personal growth community even incorporate the image of their Vision Manifesto into their vision board collage of images.

VALORIE BURTON

MISSION STATEMENT

*To create and enjoy
a fulfilling, prosperous, and generous life
and to inspire others to do the same*

VISION MANIFESTO

Relationships

I am kind. I am gentle. I am loved and I am loving. I am supported. People's lives are better when they cross paths with me. I allow others to be responsible for their choices, and me only for mine. My approach to relationships is healthy, peaceful, and reciprocal. My marriage is joyful, unified, and romantic.

Work

My work reflects my personal mission. My work improves people's lives. I have an abundance of purposeful, profitable opportunities. My work energizes and nourishes me and my family. I am getting better at what I do daily. Excellence, integrity, and faith are reflected in how I do what I do.

Finances

I am prosperous and generous. I receive blessings with gratitude and share them with humility. I do not overwork to be rich (Proverbs 23:4). Money flows my way with ease. I welcome abundance, and I am an impeccable steward of it. My family and I are debt-free. We live below our means. We use money to create meaningful experiences, passive income, and an environment of love, adventure, and purpose.

Health

I feel good daily. I nourish my body with healthy, delicious food. I move my body daily. I give myself a full night's sleep. I savor moments of rest unapologetically. I honor boundaries around my time, underpromise, and live at a peaceful pace. I drink plenty of water and enjoy how it refreshes me. I enjoy taking care of me as a way to express thanks to God for the temple I have been blessed with.

Spiritual Life

I am a vessel for God's love. I am guided by His Word. I am loved unconditionally. I am forgiven. I am an ambassador for Christ who spreads light and love in the world. I am growing in faith and living outside my comfort zone! I hear from God through my prayers, and I am courageous enough to follow what I hear. I remember that my faith is bigger than my fear and that the wisdom I need is only a prayer away. I am at peace.

Once you've written your own Vision Manifesto, read it daily as a reminder of who you want to be and how you want to show up. Post it where you'll see it. Set a daily reminder to read it. And notice how your energy shifts when you do. Dr. Laura King says that writing in the present tense about your "best possible future self" increases happiness and positive emotions, and helps you develop a positive outlook for the future.[8] This, in turn, increases your motivation to take action toward that future. Many participants in the Vision Board Challenge have included a beautiful print of their manifesto on their vision board as a written reminder of where they are headed, which seems to add energy to their intentions.

My Vision Manifesto is simple, and I read it almost daily. I keep a copy next to our elliptical machine to read when I work out. I keep another copy at my vanity where I do my hair and makeup in the mornings. I have one at my desk, too. Repetition helps us remember where we are going. So often, people set goals at the beginning of the year, put them away in a drawer or a file that never gets opened, then forget about them until the next year. By reading your Vision Manifesto daily, you paint the picture of where you intend to be at a given point in the future. Your vision will pull you forward, and when an obstacle appears, your vision will put the obstacle in perspective so it becomes easier to conquer.

How about you? What's your Vision Manifesto? Use the template on these pages, or better yet, download a fillable PDF that will allow you to type, save, and print your Vision Manifesto.[9] Don't worry about getting everything just right. Simply write the words that come to you. You can always edit it later, but first you need something on the page to edit!

Now that you've drafted your Vision Manifesto, identify images that will reflect it. The first time I created a vision board, it was old school—I clipped images from magazines. But these days, the easiest option is to do an online search for what you want. For example, if your vision includes travel to a specific country, search for images of where you want to visit. If your vision includes buying a new home, search for images that look similar to your dream home. If your vision is a business with a certain revenue or promotion to a certain position, find images or even words that reflect that vision. Then print and arrange the images in a collage on poster board. Or to create a digital vision board, you can use apps such as Canva or even your favorite presentation software. I used to love the physical vision board, but now I make mine digitally, which makes it easier to update and print.

Revisit your Vision Manifesto and vision board at least annually. Update it as you achieve elements of the vision or gain new insights that you want reflected in these tools.

Getting to the Vision: The Five Stages of Success

There's one more tool I want to share with you to help you stay focused on your vision without giving up. This powerful process begins by understanding that, no matter what goal or overall vision you're aiming for, you must move through five stages in order to achieve that vision. I developed these five stages as I was creating a personal growth membership called the Successful Women's Academy, or SWA for short. This tool can help you understand where you are on the way to a vision and what to do next to be resilient in getting there. We now teach coaches how to work with their clients to resiliently walk through these five stages to successfully navigate any goal.

Most people think of a goal and immediately jump into a discussion about what actions they need to take. Many will soon feel they are behind if they are not making progress. Then once they begin making progress, they feel frustrated when the idea doesn't go as planned. But when you understand all five stages, you understand that each stage is essential. If your initial plan isn't working perfectly and you feel behind, it's not a sign that you need to go back to the drawing board.

Remember, resilience is not just needed to navigate difficulties, but it is also needed to navigate the path to success. If you want to lose weight, you will have to be resilient when you're tempted to eat junk and skip the workout. If you want to grow your business, you'll need resilience when your big idea doesn't land with customers and you need to brainstorm again. You'll need resilience when everything seems to go your way, but somehow you still feel stressed, anxious, and as if you haven't accomplished enough! These moments offer you a nudge toward making a shift, change, or new goal that can create more fulfillment and authentic achievement. If you understand the stages, you can coach yourself calmly and resiliently to a new level of success.

Think about your vision or a specific goal. As you read through each stage, notice and then answer the coaching question. As you read the characteristics of a person in each stage, determine where you are in the process. See how Tara-Leigh navigated each step of the process while planning and executing her podcast.

STAGE 1: AWARENESS

Questions: *What's possible for me? What would be a meaningful goal?*

Characteristics: You realize that where you are is not where you want to stay. You begin wondering how things could be different. What's possible? In this phase, you are inspired and begin seeing a vision for a future that feels intriguing and exciting. As you articulate that vision, you are painting a picture of where you want to go. You don't have all the answers yet, but out of your vision you begin setting the goals to reach it.

Consider Tara-Leigh's vision. It was a nudge that came to her in prayer. She began imagining how she could make the Bible easier to understand for people in a simple format. *Maybe a 365-day podcast? Hmm.*

STAGE 2: AWAKENING

Questions: *What will it really take to achieve this vision? What fears, habits, and distractions threaten my success? What do I need to learn to be prepared to take the necessary steps toward my goal? What plan of action will enable me to reach this vision? Given the realistic plan I've come up with, do I want to pursue this vision now, do I want to pursue it at a later time, or should I drop this vision because I do not believe it will be worth the effort and resources required?*

Characteristics: You've decided what you want, and now you are taking a hard look at what it will take to get there. You are considering the circumstances, fears, thoughts, resources, and any other obstacles that could keep you from getting to your vision and goals. You know what these obstacles are because they are likely the reason you aren't at your destination already. Whereas in the Awareness stage, you use optimism to explore your possibilities and commit to your vision and goals, in the Awakening stage, you use a dose of pessimism to pinpoint the potential pitfalls and roadblocks you must overcome to bring that vison to fruition.

Now that your vision and goal are clear, you are asking yourself, *What's really holding me back?* But more importantly, you are working on a plan of action so you can push through whatever has held you back in the past. You are acknowledging the change in mindset that might be necessary. You are researching those who have achieved the vision before you and what it took for them to do so. Because you are serious about attaining the vision, you are committed to the practical planning and thoughtful repositioning necessary to set yourself up for success.

In stage 2, Tara-Leigh sketched out a plan of action and a timeline that was very aggressive. She got the equipment she needed for the podcast and a contractor to help her produce and upload the episodes. She then created a week-by-week outline of what she would teach in her six-to-eight-minute daily segments. It is at this stage that she laid out the format, which turned out to be brilliant: a 365-day chronological walk through the entire Bible.

STAGE 3: ACTION

Questions: *What next step(s) will I take from my plan and when? What will I do to stay energized?*

Characteristics: You feel butterflies and exhilaration in this stage. You might be tempted to rethink, second-guess, or even change your plans. Ignore all that. That's just fear, and now that you've been through the Awakening stage, you know what to do in the face of fear: Take action. So at this stage, you abandon overanalysis and procrastination. The planning is over, and the action has begun!

You now follow the action plan you created in stage 2, using the tools you identified to overcome your obstacles. You give yourself permission to be imperfect. Your motto in the Action stage is "Progress, not perfection!" Action is how you learn. At this point, you're having important conversations, making essential changes, and taking the necessary steps to move toward your destination.

In this stage, you feel alive because you experience the energy and adventure that come with going for it. Others are noticing. They may even be inspired. Some may be uncomfortable, but you don't let that stop you. You know that if you just keep moving forward in spite of your fears, your doubts, or even your naysayers, you will get to your finish line. Just keep going!

In stage 3, Tara-Leigh began acting on the plan she developed in stage 2. She did a lot of studying and note-taking, then narrowed each message to something succinct and meaningful. She wanted to provide a takeaway in each episode that would leave the listener with a better understanding of their faith—no small feat, but she was hyperfocused on the challenge.

STAGE 4: ADJUSTMENT

Questions: *What's working? What's not? What tweaks do I need to make to get to the finish line?*

Characteristics: One of the most powerful principles of coaching is that you learn from taking action. By the Adjustment stage, you have taken action and seen results, but you have not quite reached your vision yet. That means you need some final adjustments to get there. You see some things that are not working so you decide how to change or tweak them. And you may see other things that are working so well that you need to do them even more. In this stage, you intentionally glean lessons from the actions you've taken so far and decide what to keep doing and what to adjust.

Getting to the finish line always requires course corrections that can happen only with the wisdom you gain from having been at it for a while. There is no specific time frame for the Adjustment phase. It can take quite a while, or it can be quite quick. In some ways, it's like a second Awakening phase as you become aware of obstacles and challenges you couldn't have seen earlier in your journey. Revisit the tools you gained in stage 2 to help you be resilient and adjust your action plan as needed.

The goal here is to get to the vision. What are those last steps you need to take? What lingering fears have made you procrastinate or kept you from taking key actions? It is a point of pride to get to the Adjustment phase because it means you have persevered. With one more push, you will reach your vision.

Tara-Leigh had many opportunities to adjust that year as she completed 365 episodes. I teased her that we share the trait of time optimism—underestimating just how much time something is going to take. Tara-Leigh thought she'd spend about twenty hours a month on the podcast. Once she moved into action, she quickly entered stage 4, as she had to adjust her expectations. Her time estimate was way off. She spent about five times as much time as she expected on the series. Her modest goal of three hundred listeners a week was blown out of the water on day one, and just six weeks in, the podcast reached a million downloads. So she needed more help than she anticipated.

She also remained focused on her central vision. When she received inquiries from book publishers who assumed she had completed all 365 episodes prior to launch, she told them she couldn't respond until the end of the year and stayed focused on her podcast. She had very little personal time, but she created time for a small number of close friends. She promised others that she would reconnect with them once she'd finished the podcast's first year.

All along the way, she made adjustments. Then she focused on the goal, allowing it to pull her forward when she was exhausted. Because her faith was the top value in her life, she had a purpose-driven goal, and she felt energized knowing she was doing what she felt called to do.

STAGE 5: ACHIEVEMENT

Questions: *How will you savor your vision? How will you celebrate? What wisdom have you gained on the path to your success?*

Characteristics: You have now reached the vision you described in stage 1. You have mastered the steps it took to get to your goal. You are experiencing the benefits of arriving at your destination. You have reason to be proud and must not forget to look back and notice what it took for you to get where you are. If you got here once in one area of your life, you could get here in many other areas. Celebrate. Savor your victory. But don't forget the fundamentals that got you to where you are. They will help you maintain your success, and they may also make you aware of new opportunities, new goals, and even a new vision.

When Tara-Leigh finished the 365th episode of *The Bible Recap* podcast at the end of 2019, she took a break. She called friends and caught up. She marveled at the millions of downloads her podcast had gotten over the course of the year.

As she celebrated and savored her success, she began to ponder what was next. Given all the interest from publishers, she knew that the book project was the next vision. As she started writing, she began working through the five stages of success all over again.

When you decide to embrace resilience, notice where your eyes fall. What are you seeing in your mind's eye? If you're looking at the obstacles, you're already in trouble. But if you can stay focused on the vision—by creating a Vision Manifesto and then navigating the five stages of success—you'll be well-equipped to flourish despite the inevitable obstacles you'll face.

When you keep your eyes on the prize, you'll also be best equipped to navigate the next rule of resilience: controlling the controllable while accepting the rest.

Coach Yourself

- ▶ What is your vision?
- ▶ What are three milestones or experiences that will indicate you are on track to reaching that vision?
- ▶ What is the biggest obstacle to achieving your vision?
- ▶ What are your options for overcoming or minimizing the impact of the obstacle?
- ▶ What is your Vision Manifesto for this year—your present-tense declaration of your vision in the five key areas of your life? (Coach yourself with the Vision Manifesto questions earlier in this chapter.)
- ▶ Where will you keep your vision board and Vision Manifesto? How will you remind yourself to use them as tools to energize yourself and focus your energy when faced with an obstacle?

Try This

- ☐ Write your personal Vision Manifesto (and read it daily).
- ☐ Create a vision board and put it where you'll see it daily.
- ☐ When you get stuck, use your vision as a tool to pull you forward and put obstacles into perspective.
- ☐ As you consider your primary vision, identify which of the five stages of success you are in and what your next steps might be to move through all five stages to arrive at your vision.

SAY IT WITH ME:

"When I focus on my vision,
I put the obstacles into perspective."

RESILIENCE RULE #4

CONTROL THE CONTROLLABLE; ACCEPT THE REST

How to take responsibility, shift to an internal locus of control, and save your energy for the stuff you can do something about

---

KEY MESSAGES

- Accept responsibility so you can move from a passive mentality to a proactive one.
- Learn to operate from an internal locus of control.
- Decide to be "better, not bitter" on the other side of your challenge.

I never thought much about how powerful water is until I got my boating license and learned to navigate a thirty-four-foot powerboat on the beautiful Chesapeake Bay with its 11,000 miles of shoreline. The biggest challenge for me was the uneasy feeling of navigating a vehicle on a "road" that is ever-changing. When you're driving a car, changing direction is simple. It depends mostly on your decision to turn the vehicle using the steering wheel to move wherever you want to go. It's easy because the road is constant and steady. What fascinated me about boating is that the "road" is always moving. It's disorienting at first. It's not enough to focus only on your surroundings and vehicle; you must keep an eye on the water that is always changing beneath you.

You have very little control over what happens when you choose to travel by water. On your best days, the water is like glass, smooth and still, allowing you to glide effortlessly across its surface. On your worst days, that same water can be choppy, the current moving against you, making the ride turbulent, unpredictable, and dangerous. The best navigators always have their eyes open for clues about the conditions—tides, waves, depth, and wind speed and direction. Knowing the weather forecast is essential. Of course, you don't control any of it. What you do control is the decision whether to take the boat out given the conditions, the precautions and skill with which you operate it, and who you bring along to help. You don't control the water. But you can control the boat—when and where to go, how fast to drive, and of course, how well you maintain your craft.

The same is true of the challenges you face. The conditions you endure are constantly changing, and you must be skilled and intentional about how you navigate your environment. You have the ability to steer your life and its direction, but you must analyze the conditions and then plan and prepare accordingly so you have the best chance of successfully navigating your journey. If you don't, you may find yourself a victim of circumstances that spiral beyond your control, facing predictable turbulence and ultimately running aground or capsizing because you didn't plan ahead or heed warnings. Worse yet, you could end up adrift, going wherever the current takes you, which may land you anywhere but where you actually want to go. Many aspects of your challenges are outside your control, such as the actions and attitudes of others, situations you cannot influence, and timing. Many elements, though, are within your control, such as the effort you put in, your attitude and decisions, and how you respond.

Control What You Can

One of the most powerful rules of resilience is this: "Control the controllable; accept the rest."

There is an ease and strength that comes when you take this approach. You immediately increase your resilience because you focus your energy on the elements you have the power to do something about. You stop wasting energy and futile effort trying to change things you cannot or complaining and worrying about things that will not change. You begin asking questions like

If this is the reality, then what do I need to do to survive or thrive despite it?

What do I want to do until this unwanted reality changes?

What can I do to work around this inconvenient truth?

How can I keep myself sane/safe/productive while dealing with a situation I cannot change?

We live in a world where there is so much we do not have control over. If you like being in control, if you do not like uncertainty, and especially if you've ever been called a control freak, listen closely. If you're not careful, this mindset can become a huge obstacle to resilience.

One trap is overfocusing on things you cannot control. Think back to a time when you tried to control something or someone without success. You likely felt increased stress as feelings of fear, frustration, and even helplessness took over.

Those who are most resilient instead find what they can manage internally, even if it is small, so they can take charge of what they actually can control in a situation. This alleviates some stress and leaves them feeling empowered. It is a simple but profound shift.

At the core of my work is my lifelong curiosity about what successful, resilient people do differently. One thing they have in common is that they control the controllable and accept the rest. They don't spend too much time or energy trying to fix things they cannot. Instead, they focus on the things they can do something about that will improve their circumstances, options, and chances of success.

What's Within Your Control? What's Not?

Your locus of control is the level of control you believe that you, rather than external factors, have in determining what happens in a particular situation.[1] Individuals with a strong internal locus of control believe that their own decisions and actions largely determine what happens in their lives. So they seek to make choices and take actions that can influence positive outcomes. Those with an external locus of control tend to believe the events of their lives are the result of outside forces over which they have no control. As a result, they are less likely to see how their choices and actions can make a positive impact on the outcomes they want. They take less responsibility for their choices and often blame others for negative events in their lives.

Operating from an internal locus of control can make the emotional journey easier and ultimately lead to clarity about the right next steps. By focusing on what you can control, research shows you'll feel be more resilient, content, and successful, and you'll be more likely to take actions that actually improve your situation.[2] In fact, those who are most resilient and successful do just that. Rather than obsessing over things they have no control over—like whether someone else will change or whether the economy will improve—they focus on what they can control, including the everyday choices that will make the situation better.

The rule "Control the controllable; accept the rest" is rooted in the power of using your internal locus of control whenever possible. You act from the belief that your own actions, abilities, and decisions influence and impact what happens in your life. You take responsibility for creating a clear vision, plan, and solutions to problems. You are less likely to blame others for your challenges and more likely to own your actions and decisions rather than seeing yourself as a

ASK YOURSELF,
WHAT'S WITHIN MY CONTROL?

Some questions to consider:

- What personal boundary can I set?
- What would be a better response to this situation?
- How might I change my process?
- What shift do I need to make in how I think about this?

victim of circumstance. You are good at facing the truth, rather than pretending and defending.

What situation are you faced with right now where the outcome isn't entirely up to you? Maybe it is an opportunity you'd like to have, but others get to make the decision about whether you get it. Perhaps it's a relationship you'd like to improve, but the other person doesn't see things your way or isn't interested in getting closer. It could be a health challenge that seems so unfair, leaving you struggling not to become discouraged or frustrated.

Focus on what you can control:

You can refuse to spend energy worrying about and resisting what you can't change.

You can set a boundary to minimize the negative impact of a person you don't control.

You can set a goal to change a habit that is creating problems.

You can stop reacting to situations in ways that create strife and tension and instead choose to respond with calmness and peace.

You can turn off the TV or log off social media to keep from being reminded of anxiety-producing issues you do not control.

You can focus on what you are grateful for, work toward the best outcome possible, and choose to have faith that the situation will work together for your good.

The concept of an internal locus of control versus external locus of control is summed up by the well-known Serenity Prayer, which has been widely distributed by Alcoholics Anonymous as encouragement to those taking it step by step to win the battle over addiction: "God, grant me the serenity to accept the things I cannot change, the courage to change the things I can, and the wisdom to know the difference."

Whenever you find yourself overly focused on things you cannot change and need to shift to an internal locus of control, coach yourself with these questions:

What is within your control in this situation? What decisions, circumstances, or issues are outside of your control? Make a list.

How do you want to show up in this challenge? Identify the character traits you want to exhibit, such as courage, compassion, wisdom, or tenacity.

What would it look like for you to control the controllable? Describe it vividly.

What do you need the courage to do in this situation? When are you willing to do that?

In light of the unwanted realities and your future hopes and vision, what is the wise thing to do? When will you do it?

Acceptance Is Not Approval

Recently Sara, my curriculum designer, and I were working on a resilience training curriculum based on the ten rules in this book. As we were discussing this rule, she said, "I don't like the idea of accepting something I don't want. I want to work to change the situation."

As I listened, I realized that we often equate acceptance with approval or being happy about the situation. Yet they are not the same. There are many elements of life that we do not have the power to change, and even if we did, would it be worth spending the energy, effort, and resources to do so?

Accepting the reality that some things are beyond your control or decision-making power does not mean you approve of the situation or outcome. It simply means that you accept "what is." You acknowledge both the problem and your limitations on fixing the problem so you can make a plan for how to proceed in light of that reality. You can try to sway your adult children to make different choices, but ultimately they are the ones who decide what they will do. You can vote, but you don't choose who wins the election. You can present your case and try to influence someone making a decision, but if you're not the one who decides, you don't control the outcome.

While most people I coach resonate with the idea of controlling what they can, it's the second part of this rule—"accept the rest"—that often creates the bigger challenge. I felt this way after finally becoming pregnant with twins through in vitro fertilization (IVF) at age forty-one. Trying to conceive had been an emotional roller-coaster ride. Millions of women get pregnant by accident, many even while using birth control, but without the medical intervention of IVF, conceiving proved elusive for me. During the grueling process, it was hard to stay positive in light of the many disappointments and the physical toll of constant appointments and tests and administering shots to myself in the abdomen or thigh on a daily basis.

Pregnancy was the goal. And it was a dream come true. It felt surreal when it finally happened. We had two healthy embryos transferred successfully. My husband and I were overjoyed. My bonus daughters were excited. Our parents were thrilled. I'll never forget when we told my dad that both embryos were implanted successfully. "There are *two*?!" he asked over the phone, his voice rising with such excitement about the thought of twin grandbabies. If all went well, I'd give birth in July.

But all did not go well. The unexpected happened. It never occurred to me that we'd finally arrive at the goal of pregnancy only to have it snatched away. But that's what happened.

When I got up that Saturday morning, I knew something was wrong but told myself everything would be okay. When we called the doctor's office, they told us to come in right away. It was a fifty-minute drive without traffic. As soon as Jeff and I got there, they did an ultrasound. The results confirmed the worst news. There were no heartbeats.

I felt numb. Blindsided. Speechless.

I'll never forget driving home from the doctor's office in complete silence, our only words spoken through the touch of each other's hands, held tightly as they rested on the console between us. We were in shock.

It took time to grieve and process my loss. And I gave myself the time. "Accepting the rest" can be heart-wrenching. I didn't understand why this had happened, but I accepted the reality. I leaned on my faith. I truly believed that if I were meant to have children biologically, I would. For some reason, that was not my path. "Lean not on your own understanding," Proverbs 3:5 advises, and I meditated on those words often.

Acceptance also freed me to discover a place of peace and a path forward that offered unexpected blessings. I knew I didn't want to go through IVF again. I'd decided before we even began treatment that I would do only one round because I didn't want to look back in regret later in life if I didn't try it. But I just didn't have it in me to do it again. I accepted that motherhood would likely not come through me giving birth. My husband and I had agreed before we married that we also wanted to adopt. And the following year, the door opened and we became parents to our son. Accepting the rest can mean acknowledging realities we'd rather not, but when we do, we can then open our minds to the opportunities that come with a different path. In letting go, I found peace. I found love and the child I believe with all my heart we were meant to raise.

Maybe "accepting the rest" for you involves a challenge at work or in a relationship, a financial or health reality. For example, if you've ever been laid off due to downsizing, you likely did not control your employer's decision to cut your position or the economic conditions that led to that decision. You might second-guess why your position was eliminated while a coworker's was not. You may not want to accept it, but if you focus your energy on anger or if you beat yourself up for not taking steps that may have saved your job, you steal energy from your efforts to recover, refocus, and pivot toward the future.

If you are dealing with a difficult person you keep expecting to change, you might give them advice about how to change and all the reasons they should. In the end, you'll likely discover that your efforts are in vain. When you expect people to do what they cannot or will not do, you will be disappointed. If you implement the "control the controllable" rule, you'll decide whether to accept their limitations or make adjustments to how you handle those limitations. That might mean setting boundaries, changing what you do or don't do with them, or removing yourself from the situation. You don't have to approve of their behavior to accept the reality that you cannot change them. It takes courage to accept a reality you don't want, but by doing so you'll open the door to new and authentic solutions.

After Acceptance, What's Next?

I have often shared a story of resilience that has been so inspiring to me—my own mother's journey. It has included disheartening challenges that led my mom to make a heart-wrenching but resilient decision. Her choice exemplifies the power of the rule to "control the controllable; accept the rest."

When my mom was forty-nine, she suffered a ruptured brain aneurysm one evening while she and I were talking on the phone. It was devastating. After emergency brain surgery and two months in the hospital, she came home and spent every day trying to regain the most basic of physical abilities, such as walking, talking, seeing clearly, and swallowing. The doctors told me there was a 90 percent chance she'd never swallow again and would have to be fed through a tube in her stomach. If she walked, she'd always have a limp, they said. Her vision? Well, that was too hard to predict. Technically, she could see, but what she saw was simultaneously double or triple and spinning. Worse than not being able to speak or walk or swallow, she said, was opening her eyes and seeing only chaos.

With tenacity and persistence like I'd never seen up close, my mother slowly recovered most of her abilities over the next few years. For instance, she went from not being able to sit up on her own to getting around in a wheelchair by her fiftieth birthday. From there, she learned to shuffle forward one step at a time, then take multiple steps with the help of a walker, and finally walk with a cane! Soon after, as long as she focused, she was able to walk on her own.

But that progress lasted only a few years before something perplexing began to happen. Walking became harder again. The muscles in her right thigh began to tighten. It became hard for her to bend her knee. Stumbling became a constant problem. She tried using a cane again, but it was hard to coordinate her movements, which caused her to stumble even more. Soon she was using a walker again, and we were back to frequent doctor appointments to try to figure out why her mobility was regressing.

No one seemed to have an answer, but the problem continued to get worse. We traveled far away to renowned clinics seeking help. The answer after multiple tests? "It's a medical mystery." The consensus seemed to be that because she was only forty-nine when the ruptured aneurysm occurred, her body had been able to compensate for this problem. But as she got older, the brain and body were not as able to do so. That explanation seemed plausible, but my mother felt deep down that was not the reason for her decline. She believed something else was going on. But what was it?

After nearly a decade of seeing multiple specialists, we found a neurologist who insisted there was an answer and he would find it. The likelihood of an explanation that had nothing at all to do with the aneurysm seemed quite unlikely. To put this into context, having a ruptured brain aneurysm is a very rare event. It turns out that one in fifty Americans has an existing unruptured brain aneurysm, meaning they have a blood vessel that has ballooned but is causing no symptoms.[3] It can remain that way for decades without a problem. Only 0.01 percent of the population experiences a rupture in any given year. My mom was part of that 0.01 percent. Half of those who have a rupture die from it within three months; half of those die within mere hours.[4]

The neurologist initially diagnosed her with a very rare condition, spastic paraplegia, and for over five years, she proceeded with treatment for that disease. But recently, tests revealed she was misdiagnosed. The search for answers continues, and as of this writing, she is fighting every day to keep walking. But it's hard. She has fallen. Her leg buckles unexpectedly. She cannot walk around the house without holding on to something. She gets tired faster. Her tongue feels heavy, which can make speaking exhausting and difficult. So we tend to keep our conversations shorter than we used to.

One summer evening my mother and I were chatting in our kitchen as my husband, Jeff, was cooking one of his gourmet meals. "He's making something called Coquilles St. Jacques," I explained to my mom. "It's got scallops, and it's creamy with crisp breadcrumbs on top."

Jeff loves to cook. Feeding people is his way of loving them. And my mom loves good food but does not love cooking. "Well, you know, whenever Jeff is cooking up something special like that," Mom said, "save me a little bit, and I'll come by and get it."

My husband's immediate response? "Well, if you lived with us, you could just come to the kitchen and have some."

Jeff was half joking, knowing it was a sensible idea but also knowing her answer to the suggestion. As she always had before, she immediately shut down the idea. The lighthearted conversation took on a suddenly serious tone. "No, I am not moving. I like living by myself, and I am not moving in with y'all."

My mother had been adamant for years that she would *never* live with us. She gave me elaborate plans for how she would manage to live by herself in her home if and when she was no longer able to walk. So I wasn't surprised that, after Jeff made that comment, she made it clear that moving was not an option she would consider.

The next day, I stopped by her house to bring the food. On my way out, I felt led to repeat Jeff's sentiment. She assured me she would be staying put, but this time, something about the idea seemed to linger with her. In her quiet time in the coming days, she prayed about it. And something in her spirit was nudging her to soften her rigid stance. Being the woman of faith that she is, a message from God is probably the only thing that could have changed her mind. After years of insisting that she would never give up the independence of living in her own home alone, a different answer emerged.

A few days later, I opened my email to a message from my mom with the subject line "Being realistic." In it, she told me that because of how quickly the spastic paraplegia was progressing, it didn't make sense to decline our offer to come live with us. She said she had to be realistic about her situation and shift her mindset.

It took a great deal of courage in the face of vulnerability to confront the truth that her condition was getting worse, and living alone could prove detrimental and even dangerous. Accepting the reality of an unwanted circumstance is hard. In some instances, it can feel crushing. I don't know all of the thoughts that have gone through my mom's head, but I know the ones that have gone through mine. It hurts to imagine her not being able to walk.

It's so unfair. And yet I know that life often seems that way. But it feels especially unfair when a person with a heart of gold who is full of faith and has been generous to so many after enduring so much has to deal with two rare, incurable health problems. As her daughter, I feel deep sadness and the kind of perplexity that wants to ask, "Why my mom?" But the reality is, there is never a satisfying answer to that question. Life is unfair. Our job is to accept that reality and then deal with it so we can survive, and even thrive, in spite of that fact. Denying that truth could make a bad situation worse.

The truth, once she accepted it, empowered my mom to take responsibility and make a decision that ensures she has more support and is in a safer space with family in the event of a fall or other problem. While she does not control the symptoms or their progression, she had the power to make a decision that put her in a better position to manage the risks of those symptoms.

She controlled the controllable and accepted the rest. Like a boater sizing up the forecast and water conditions, she realized that her progressive illness meant the waters were choppier and she was far from the shore should she need help. Moving in with us was like moving into a bigger, stronger boat with a helpful crew in tow. It didn't mean there would be no danger; it meant she had more protective resources to navigate inevitable challenges. She used adaptive skills, including thought awareness, flexibility, faith, and prayer, to gain the courage to come up with a game plan for her future that would help her navigate the physical challenges.

Learned Helplessness

What happens when you don't embrace an internal locus of control? How does that impact your resilience? When you operate from an external locus of control, believing your fate is entirely in the hands of others, you are powerless and helpless. What's the point of trying? Of planning? Of looking for options that can improve your situation or get you to the goal? When you have an external locus of control, you feel your outcomes are at the mercy of what others do and you have little control over any of it. When you embrace this way of thinking, nothing you do really matters because other people and circumstances control what happens in your life; you are simply a victim of their decisions and choices.

This belief system can slide toward the extreme and become learned helplessness, a term coined by Dr. Martin E. P. Seligman and researchers at the University of Pennsylvania in 1967.[5] According to the American Psychological Association, learned helplessness occurs when "repeated exposure to uncontrollable stressors results in individuals failing to use any control options that may later become available."[6] Past experiences of being unable to change a situation have cemented a belief that their efforts won't matter, so people no longer attempt to better their circumstances, even when change is possible. The past experiences don't even have to be their own: They may assume others' experiences will also apply to them, or they may choose to adopt the negative beliefs of others—whether parents, friends, or coworkers—for themselves.

When you operate from an external locus of control, you can often feel powerless or victimized, or waste a great deal of energy doing things that don't change your circumstances while believing that they actually can. As a result, you end up feeling stuck.

As a result, you blame those whom you believe have power for your life circumstances. You believe you have no responsibility for how you show up. Whatever happens is someone else's fault. Of course, sometimes things do happen through no fault of your own, but when the default response for your behavior is blaming others, you may be using that blame to absolve yourself of any responsibility.

Showing up with a good attitude? Not your responsibility. Doing what is within your power to do? Nope, not your responsibility either. Making *some* progress, even if you are unable to meet the entire goal? Not worth it. When all problems are the fault of someone or something else, you can fall into the trap of feeling sorry for yourself and blaming others rather than taking responsibility for what you can control.

Eventually, due to feelings of powerlessness brought on by the inability to do anything about the forces beyond your control, you give up. You come to the conclusion that nothing you do matters.

The result of learned helplessness is that you become apathetic. Motivation is sapped. This is more likely to happen when you've been through a series of negative events, disappointments, or circumstances. Multiple adversities can wear out your resources and thinking, making it hard to stay resilient. Notice if this happens. Talk to someone with a history of resilience and a spirit of encouragement so you can get a different perspective. Or get counseling if you can. With intention and practice, you can unlearn a helplessness habit and learn to embrace an internal locus of control.

Learn to Discern What's Yours to Control

The problem of an external locus of control is not just about refusing to take responsibility, though. It can also manifest in futilely focusing your energy on trying to change people or circumstances that simply will not change. It's like running feverishly on a treadmill, increasing your speed to 8 mph and believing that if you just keep going, you'll actually travel eight miles! You strategize and plan, try different approaches and angles, still sure you will get to your vision eight miles down the road. But you won't. And you never will. And that's because a treadmill is not a mode of transportation. And there

Focusing too much on what you have no control over will sabotage your resilience.

is nothing you can do to turn it into one. It is essential that you have a realistic view of what you actually can control. Focusing too much on what you have no control over will sabotage your resilience.

There are some things in life you simply cannot control, for example,

- decisions that are not yours to make (though you can try to influence the decision and decide your best course of action once it's been made)
- others' personal growth (though you can cheer on their efforts)
- whether others like or love you (though you control whether you like and love yourself and others)
- the behavior and reactions of others (though you control your reactions to them)
- what others think, feel, or believe (though you control how you listen and respond)
- the thoughts that show up (though you get to choose which ones to dwell on)
- the outcome of your goals (though you control the effort and consistency you put in)
- getting older and aging (though you can take care of yourself)
- the existence of pain and suffering (though you can contribute to or alleviate some of it)
- how others treat you (though you can control how you respond)
- what others do (though you get to decide whether to follow suit or set boundaries)
- what already happened (though the past is a fact, you can choose what to do in the present)

A key to becoming more resilient is taking control of what you can. That may mean accepting that you have less control over other people than you'd like. Even so, your close relationships are extremely valuable; in fact, they are one of your key protective resources. What are the others? Recognizing *all* the tools available to you, whether you're faced with an unexpected challenge or an exciting opportunity, is key to becoming more resilient.

Coach Yourself

- In what situation(s) do you need to apply the concept "Control the controllable; accept the rest" right now?
- What's within your control?
- What would it look like to "control the controllable" right now?
- What's out of your control?
- What would it look like to accept that reality and reclaim your energy?
- Which needs to shift—your vision or just your approach?

Try This

- ☐ Identify one to three pressing scenarios where others' decisions or behaviors impact your resilience.
- ☐ Use the coaching questions to take responsibility and shift your focus to what you can control. Then make a plan of action.
- ☐ Decide when you will move forward on your action plan.

SAY IT WITH ME:

"Ease and strength come when I control the controllable and accept the rest."

RESILIENCE RULE #5

RALLY YOUR RESOURCES

Cultivate resources and relationships before you need them so you can tap into them to get unstuck.

KEY MESSAGES

- Personal resources make resilience easier, so assess and build the right ones.
- Strong relationships are a foundational resource for your personal resilience.
- Be willing to ask for help.

Several years after Michelle Williams stepped onto the scene as the newest member of the super-successful Destiny's Child, the group disbanded. She had found success as a solo gospel artist and Broadway actress even while the group was together, and she continued on that path, starring in *The Color Purple*, *Aida*, and *Chicago*, among other productions. But Michelle says her proudest moment of resilience came during a dark time.

In late 2017, Michelle began to feel symptoms of depression, something she'd struggled with previously. By the following year, she knew what she was experiencing this time was different and more intense. She felt hopeless, and thoughts of death were frequent.

"I knew I needed help when I got too comfortable with the idea of death," Michelle explains. "I played *Let's Make a Deal* with God, like, *I've already lived a life, I can go now. Is there something behind door #4? What more is there for me to be doing here?*" The thoughts were persistent.

Despite success in her gospel career and acclaimed acting performances on Broadway and television, Michelle recognized that the hopes and expectations she had for her personal life weren't being met. She'd had a public breakup. She felt misunderstood. And she knew she couldn't climb out of this dark hole by herself. She decided to ask for help and checked herself into an in-patient mental health facility.

"I was resilient when I walked into the facility," she says with conviction, pointing out that the resilience came when she admitted she had a problem and decided to reach out for help. Her attitude and actions exemplify Resilience Rule #5: "Rally your resources."

When I first began studying resilience, the idea that our support system can make or break our ability to persevere was one of the most intriguing concepts to me. Typically, we think of our support system as relationships we can rely on in a challenge, whether to help us land a job after a layoff or lend a listening ear when loss or stress feels overwhelming. And while relationships are probably the most important element in our support system, we often don't consider resources like access to money, education, experience, and even physical health.

Our support system can make or break our ability to persevere.

While the adaptive skills of how you think, plan, and adjust mentally are internal, your support system is made up of the external resources of relationships and life circumstances that impact whether and how quickly you can navigate challenges. Resources refer to anything tangible that will protect you from the negative impact of challenges or adversity and make it easier to navigate them.

Bigger Challenges Require Bigger Support Systems

Research shows that the bigger the challenge, the bigger the support system needed to successfully navigate the obstacle or achieve the goal.[1] You probably have more resources than you think, and you likely have many opportunities to cultivate resources so that you are better equipped to be resilient through future challenges. Whether you need to reach out for help because your mental health is suffering (as Michelle did years ago), or you have a big career or financial goal that will take mentorship, training, and new connections, you need a support system to be resilient. What would it look like for you to rally your resources in your current challenge? Whatever you're facing today, you can dramatically increase your resilience by doing three things:

1. **Cultivate and build a strong support system of protective resources.** Building resources that can protect against or at least reduce the impact of storms is essential to resilience. Many are generated by the preventive choices you make—saving money, investing in your education and skills, setting boundaries and avoiding toxic relationships, nurturing strong relationships, and taking good care of your health. These preventive choices help you cultivate a strong support system of resources you can access as the need arises.

2. **Watch for additional outside resources you can tap into.** It's not particularly effective to have resources if you don't notice them or use them when needed. In addition, sometimes you have to be proactive and seek out additional support. It usually won't just appear on your doorstep. To be resilient, open your eyes to potential resources in your community that you may not have recognized. Also, be willing to reach out for help when you need it. This is what Michelle did when she faced debilitating depression that threatened to upend her life and career.

3. **Expand and diversify your relational network.** We know that people tend to help those in their existing networks, and we also know that people's networks most often look like them—in terms of culture, gender, age, and economic status. And while people naturally behave in these ways, you have the freedom to move beyond your natural networks of

relationships. And this can be particularly important when it comes to rallying your resources.

When things go wrong, your most important resource is strong relationships. You need people in your life who care for you, with whom you can be real, imperfect, and honest about how you're really doing. Michelle first reached out to a close friend to talk about her struggle and her intense feeling that she needed professional help. This friend affirmed and encouraged Michelle to seek mental health treatment. Michelle knew she needed that level of support to get better, so she checked into a place that could provide that. By tapping into the protective resource of a strong friendship and wise counsel, and then accessing professional-level expertise and support, Michelle was able to enlist the resources she needed to recover.

Authenticity Gives You Permission to Reach Out

Even though the Hollywood image of resilience is often portrayed by superheroes who strike out on their own to defeat overwhelming challenges and a legion of bad guys—think James Bond, Wonder Woman, or Superman—the truth is, the most resilient people don't go it alone. They intentionally cultivate relationships and resources to draw on when faced with a challenge. Of course, that requires a bit of humility. If you're afraid of rejection or the disapproval of others, you may resist this rule at first. I know I did. It's almost as though admitting the problem makes it suddenly more real—and that can be scary. But if you don't let the fear intimidate you, the sobering reality can jolt you to start looking for solutions. When you "don't pretend, don't defend" (see Resilience Rule #7), you can rally resources you'd otherwise insist you don't need.

The first step is to tell yourself the truth; admit that the challenge you face is both serious and important to overcome. Then figure out what resources you can lean on to overcome it.

When Michelle realized she needed professional help, she knew her situation wouldn't remain private. Instead, it would become public knowledge, maybe even a source of gossip. Because she was a celebrity, not only would her friends and family know, but the tabloids would pry. She wondered, *What will they say? What will fans think?* She was in the midst of performing in a Broadway show, so she also wondered, *Will this end my career?* In short, *Will I be rejected?* The answers to those persistent, fear-mongering questions were the same for her as they would be for you and me: *Maybe.* And she was willing to deal with the fallout.

Michelle decided that getting help outweighed the threat of tabloid stories or gossip. She jokes that her mother says she shares TMI (too much information). But, as she says, "TMI saved my life!" Her transparency in admitting she wasn't well was a turning point. "It was freeing," she explains. Pretending she was okay wouldn't make her okay.

"I was resilient when I didn't care if anyone saw me," she says. "I told myself, *I need help. I'm going to come out better.*"

Michelle rallied multiple resources. She called on family and friends for emotional support. She called on professional therapists. She used financial resources to get in-patient treatment. And she leaned heavily on her faith, believing that all things could work together for her good. Her faith gave her hope that if she faced the problem head-on, something better was on the horizon. A deeper purpose might even emerge from it.

On the other side of her depression, Michelle found that new purpose: speaking out about mental health, encouraging others to be courageous and honest about their struggles and then to get the help that can change everything. She wrote the book *Checking In: How Getting Real about Depression Saved My Life—and Can Save Yours.*[2] You might even say Michelle rallied her resources when she reached out to me, looking for feedback and insights about public speaking.

As it turned out, we live near each other and formed a friendship. That led Michelle to realize that coaching could be a powerful skill in the mental health advocacy work she's doing. She became certified as a coach through The CaPP Institute, in addition to the speaking, podcasting, and writing she does. This work has turned her pain into purpose, allowing her to use her celebrity platform in a powerful way. Rallying your resources multiplies your options for solving challenges and often opens doors of opportunity you might not otherwise hear about.

Resources May Show Up Unexpectedly

When you have friends and family who can help, money to fix problems, the ability to hire outside help, or access to information to help solve challenges, it makes recovering from setbacks and seizing opportunities unfold faster and with more ease.

For example, when you're trying to determine the best approach on that proposal you're writing, having someone who's been there as a sounding board can mean the difference between landing the client or not. When you're a single parent, you can manage unexpected schedule changes better when you have an adult family member as a backup on the days when you can't pick your child up from school. When the unexpected happens and you land in the hospital and your medical insurance covers everything, you experience the comfort of that protective resource. When you really want to move ahead in your career and you're the first in your family to have a corporate job, the mentor or sponsor in your organization who gives you the inside scoop on what to do or not do can help you climb the ladder.

But what do you do when your support system is weak, when you don't have the money for professional help or family to fall back on? It's hard. It can be discouraging, and you can feel like giving up. It's okay to have all of those feelings, but you must make a decision to use what you have available. Control the controllable and accept where you are right now. What's the controllable?

- *Your attitude.* When you lack resources, it is even more important that you focus on your internal locus of control. It is easy to feel like a victim of circumstances who is unlucky and beholden to the external cards stacked against you. But the most powerful thing you can do is accept what is (not approve of it, but accept your current reality), and then ask, *In light of my current circumstances, what can I do to improve my situation?* Embracing an attitude of gratitude, focus, and persistence can take you to a new level. When I wanted to finish college and my parents' divorce caused their finances to take a turn for the worse, I had to get creative. I had a vision of getting an education without drowning in debt, so I looked for opportunities that gave me access to that. As a result, I turned down offers from dream schools I wanted to attend because they had a price tag I couldn't afford.

- *Your priority.* If there was only one objective you could meet right now, what would it be? Focus on the most important goal, the one that most reflects your values and will activate your grit to keep going until you reach it. Maybe it is getting out of your current housing or job situation, giving your children a healthy environment to grow up in, or gaining the freedom to manage your time the way you want. Whatever the priority, get clear about it and the choices you can make now to move in that direction.
- *Your ability to gain access to new resources.* You may not have all the resources you need right now, but with some thought and research, you may discover resources you didn't know existed or that you've overlooked. For example, I have referred several friends and family members who wanted to buy a house but lacked the necessary down payment to the Neighborhood Assistance Corporation of America (NACA), which offers a program to help first-time homebuyers get their finances in order and buy a home with no down payment and below-market interest rates. When a friend told me about it years ago, it seemed too good to be true, but it is real—so I started passing on the info. Whether it's scholarships for education, local programs for people in your situation, or employee benefits you haven't explored, do your homework and seek out available resources you might not have known existed.

What Resources Make a Strong Support System?

Once you see your support system as something you can build and the importance of intentionally developing resources as a strategy for resilience and success, you'll begin filtering your decisions through this lens. Suddenly, you realize that so many of your life's choices either build resilience or weaken it. The friendships and relationships you choose, the money and health choices you make, and even the battles you decide are worth fighting—all impact your resilience.

STRENGTHEN YOUR INTERPERSONAL CONNECTIONS AND OTHER RESOURCES

How strong is your support system right now? For each area below, estimate how confident you feel about increasing your resilience with the resources you have:

1. **Meaningful personal connections.** Your personal relationships include family and friends, of course, but you also gain a sense of community from neighbors, your place of worship, and other organizations you belong to. Close relationships give you a sense of safety and belonging that builds confidence. The emotional and often physical support they offer also make it more likely that you will recover from hardship. Those closest to you are the first place to go for support, whether dealing with bad news or celebrating good news. In fact, supportive personal relationships are the single greatest predictor of resilience.[3] Build and nurture them intentionally.

2. **Wise counsel and coaching.** Make sure that among your personal relationships, you have insightful people in your circle who share your values, listen well, and can be a sounding board. Whether it is a friend and the two of you serve in this role for each other, or you hire a coach, advisor, or trainer, intentionally build relationships with people who have expertise, good

judgment, and your best interests at heart. Think of those you trust as your personal advisory board because of their wisdom, care, and consistency. Their perspective can be so valuable as you navigate challenges and choose your next steps.

STRENGTHEN YOUR INTERPERSONAL CONNECTIONS

Who are the people who give you a sense of safety and belonging?

Who are the ones on your "personal advisory board"?

What could you do to strengthen the significant professional relationships in your life?

What are the financial resources you can count on now? Which do you want to develop?

When you think about the vision or challenge in front of you, what training or education do you have that can help you? Is there any training or education that you are lacking? How might you obtain it?

3. **Meaningful professional connections.** Significant professional relationships help you build career and financial resilience. These connections include former and current colleagues, coworkers, customers, mentors, and bosses. They give you meaning and perspective, but they can also help you learn and grow, discover opportunities, and bounce back from setbacks better when you are connected. Fostering these connections through goodwill, a strong work ethic, and reciprocal assistance can strengthen your resilience and give you leverage when navigating challenges.

4. **Financial and employment resources.** When you begin to see your finances not just in terms of what you would like to buy or where you would like to travel, but as a resource that helps you navigate uncertainty with ease and face challenges with more stability, it shifts your perspective on how to manage your money. Your employment provides a financial resource beyond just your salary. Financially impactful benefits may

come with employment, such as insurance, paid leave, retirement plans, training, and other opportunities to increase your skills and earning power.

5. **Education and training.** It is a powerful resource to have the training or expertise to land certain jobs, operate businesses, or even understand how to do certain tasks that might be needed to overcome a challenge. Education can be formal, but it can also be informal. Online classes, learning from someone who knows, and—my favorite—reading relevant books can all help you navigate challenges and adversity.

GATHER NEEDED INFORMATION

When I self-published my first book many years ago, people asked me how I learned to do it. "This book looks as good as some of my favorite bestsellers at the bookstore!" they told me. I always responded with a chuckle. Then I explained, "I bought a book about how to write a book, and I did what it said. Then I bought a book about publicizing a book, and I followed the instructions. It worked! Finally, I bought a book about how to get a literary agent, I did what it said, wrote to six agents who seemed like a fit, and landed one." I'm not saying it's always easy to implement what you learn from training or a book, but it is often easy to find information when you look for it. Whether you need strategies for overcoming a health challenge or ideas on how to improve your executive presence or save your marriage, seek out informational resources.

As I discovered when wanting to write a book, sometimes we don't possess the required resources, but all we need is to gain access to the right information. Such tools come in many forms. For example, you may work for an organization that gives you access to publications, mentors, or conferences you wouldn't otherwise have. Or you may know people or be part of a community that offers you access to some of the resources that follow.

1. **Experience.** We've all heard that experience is the best teacher, and when you are intentional about learning the lessons, it is a powerful protective resource. Once you gain experience, you know what to expect in certain situations so you can prepare well. You're often less anxious because you've been there before, and you may have insights that enable you to be more effective in a crisis or challenge. Experience also enables you to seize future opportunities.

2. **Environment.** Being in the right place and around the right people can help you navigate challenges. How well does your environment support your vision and the challenges you face? If you're in a detrimental or toxic environment that forces you to deal with negativity and manipulation, it will be harder to navigate challenges. Whether in your professional setting, home environment, or even geographic location, be intentional about setting yourself up for success and resilience. For example, when I started my life over, I chose to move to an area where I have a lot of family. Because I knew my vision included marriage and children, I wanted to live in a place where I might meet someone who wanted to live near my family.

3. **Health.** If anything can stop everything in your life in a heartbeat, it is a health crisis. Good health is a protective resource, so assess yours and then explore ways to maintain or improve it. Then take your health plan seriously, recognizing that strong health is a priceless treasure. If you have health complications, consider not only how you might rally your resources to lessen those difficulties, but also how you might give yourself grace and adjust expectations so that you don't make the journey harder than it has to be. This is a process, as the loss of one's health is not just a physical challenge, but an emotional one as well.

How Do You Cultivate a Stronger Support System?

The first step to strengthening your support system is to take an inventory of the resources you already have to weather storms or navigate the road to success. Your second step is to make choices that build your resources, reducing your risk of future problems and challenges.

Rallying your resources taps into the second and third pillars of resilience. Remember that the second pillar includes the resources you currently have available, and the third pillar is established through preventive choices you make to build your resources for both unexpected and planned future challenges and goals. For example, as part of your financial resources, you might ensure that you include savings that will help you through current challenges, and that you also make the preventive choice to increase your retirement savings rate. You might take note that you've got a couple of close friends to lean on as you sort through a relationship challenge you've been having with your child, and also decide to tap into your health plan coverage to seek professional counseling around the issue because you want to learn the skills to navigate these persistent challenges better in the future. In other words, you want to identify the resources you have now *and* make choices to shore up your resources to prevent or reduce future challenges.

For each of the protective resources above, there are two simple steps for you to take.

1. ASSESS YOUR SUPPORT SYSTEM

How strong is it right now? Take a simple inventory of your support system. On a scale of 1 to 10 (with 1 being not at all and 10 being very well), rate how well-equipped you are with each of the following resources.

As you assign a number, consider your current vision and the challenges you want to better navigate. What is the threat posed by those risks and challenges? What vision do you want to reach?

- meaningful personal connections and community
- professional connections and work advantages

- environment
- financial resources
- education and training
- experience
- health
- access to information and resources

2. STRENGTHEN YOUR SUPPORT SYSTEM

What will you do to build it? Next, identify steps you can take to strengthen each of these resources. These preventive choices will help you reduce or eliminate certain stressors in the future. For example, you might make automatic deductions into an investment account to build your financial cushion, or you might commit to regular phone calls or outings with people you want to build a relationship with. Or you could commit to going to certain conferences to build your network. You could decide to go to therapy for six months or get a coach to reach an important goal. Perhaps you will commit to finding and reading books that close your growth gap in a particular area.

What are you willing to do to create, maintain, or cultivate your resources? If you decide to build some of your resources on autopilot, what do you need to put in place consistently?

1. Meaningful personal connections and community________

    ____

2. Professional connections and work advantages ___________

    ____

3. Environment _____________________________________

    ____

4. Financial resources_______________________________

    ____

5. Education, information, and training ______________________________

6. Experience ______________________________

7. Health ______________________________

8. Access to information and resources ______________________________

When my mother suffered a ruptured brain aneurysm, the support system she'd built with these eight crucial resources helped her navigate this challenge in significant ways. Although disability compensation, which covered two-thirds of her income, would kick in ninety days after the brain surgery, she needed more than what her own sick leave and vacation days would cover. So when a friend sent out an email to coworkers, seeking assistance, these coworkers donated over three hundred hours of vacation time to help cover that ninety-day gap. For example, a man my mother had been kind to but had never officially met offered her forty hours of his own paid vacation time. And what led to these resources? Personal relationships.

My mother explains that my father's military career opened the door to her career when she was twenty-eight. When she started at the company, he insisted that she opt in to the comprehensive disability plan, pointing out that it was worth the cost if something were to ever go wrong. The close friend from work who coordinated the donation of vacation time was the same friend who, along with one other coworker, rushed to the ICU waiting room at 2 a.m. when I told her my mother was in brain surgery. My mother's siblings came to Texas within twenty-four hours, and then rotated time in Texas to support her during the two months she was in the hospital. Because we lived in the same city, I moved in to take care of my mom when she got out of the hospital. I was able to advocate on her behalf when the hospital care plan called for my mom to move to a nursing home and again when her insurance company denied in-home speech, physical, and occupational therapy. Without her support system, a situation that was already devastating would have been much worse.

Resilient People Do Not Go It Alone

All the resources are important, but since relationships are the most foundational resource, let's spend the rest of the chapter talking about how relationships build or weaken your resilience.

The most resilient people do not go it alone. They are discerning about who they enter into relationship with, making preventive choices that keep a strong boundary around their relationship life. If you think back over your biggest challenges that you ultimately triumphed over, there is a good chance that other people were intertwined with your victory. It wasn't a lone victory. Someone contributed an idea, sat with you and worked through a problem, or cheered you on from the sidelines. Relationships can impact your other resources in dramatic ways, both positive and negative. For example, toxic relationships can affect your physical and mental health, ruin other relationships, undermine career and financial opportunities, and create an anxious and contentious environment that makes it hard to be productive.[4] On the other hand, one strong relationship can inspire you to step out in faith, take a smart risk, or open a door of opportunity to the ideal job, the ideal spouse, or the investment that changes your financial trajectory. Research even confirms that children who have at least one positive, pivotal adult relationship are much more likely to experience resilience and success.[5]

THE POWER OF ONE STABLE, COMMITTED RELATIONSHIP

I met Chaunté Lowe when we shared the stage speaking at Maxwell Leadership's Day to Grow Conference. I was struck by her humility, energy, and vision, as well as the inner resilience that earned her a spot at four consecutive Olympic Games in 2004, 2008, 2012, and 2016, plus multiple national and international medals, championships, and records. Chaunté, who is also the American women's high jump record-holder, first set the goal of becoming an Olympian after watching the legendary Flo Jo—Florence Griffith Joyner—compete in the 1988 Olympics. Chaunté was just four years old at the time, but she declared that vision boldly. She began competing in track and field even before high school but says her turning point as an athlete came when her family moved. She landed at a high school in Riverside, California, where the coach took an approach to high jump that would change the trajectory of her life.

Chaunté explains, "I was on a high school team where the coach's goal was always a state championship. It was God's divine plan. There was turmoil in my life and we moved, and this happened to be my new high school. The coach knew what it took." He understood what it would take to make it to the pinnacle of world competition. "Previous coaches knew the basics, like how to run on your toes or swing your arms," she explains. But with this new coach, she says, "It wasn't just technique. It was a strategy and a system. I had to make the conscious decision to show up every day knowing it was going to hurt, but if I did what he said, it'd be worth it."

The impact Chaunté's coach had on her life tracks with what researchers at the Center on the Developing Child at Harvard University point out:

> No matter the source of hardship, the single most common factor for children who end up doing well is having the support of at least one stable and committed relationship with a parent, caregiver, or other adult. These relationships are the active ingredient in building resilience: they provide the personalized responsiveness, scaffolding, and protection that can buffer children from developmental disruption.[6]

Chaunté's coach had guided numerous athletes to state and national championships, and he knew that colleges would be watching those athletes at the state championships in California. Following his guidance and training, Chaunté won the National Scholastic Indoor Track Championships twice and led her school's team to the state team championships with her contributions in high jump, long jump, and triple jump. Soon colleges came calling, and Chaunté won a scholarship to Georgia Tech. The turning point, she says, came when a coach taught her the strategy for performing at a championship level, something she had not learned elsewhere.

WHEN YOU ARE OPEN TO SHARING, YOU ARE OPEN TO RECEIVING

The impact one man had on Chaunté's life resonates with an experience I had as well.

After my parents' divorce and the loss of our home, there was no college fund. I'd had a full ride my first year of college and completed my second year at a California community college, where I could take as many hours as I wanted for a grand total of $60 per semester. I still can't explain how California could offer that in the 1990s, but I am grateful!

For my final two years of college, I'd been offered partial scholarships to Pepperdine and the University of Southern California. Either way, I'd still have to take out a significant amount in student loans. While trying to figure out where to go on my limited financial resources, I remembered something that could solve my problem. Because my father had kept his first duty station, Florida, as his official state of residency on his military records, I had access to in-state tuition there and discovered a financially feasible option for college. I decided to transfer to the Panama City campus of Florida State University. I'd been born at Tyndall Air Force Base in Panama City, and I knew about the FSU campus in that city because my parents had attended part-time when we lived there—although it had been the University of West Florida extension campus back then.

I enrolled over the summer, but when it was time to register for the fall semester, something happened that changed everything. As I met with a man—I have no idea who he was, perhaps an assistant dean or academic counselor—to discuss my class options, he casually asked questions about my background and how I ended up at the Panama City campus.

That made him even more curious. "So you don't have any family here, your parents are in California and Colorado, you're nineteen and living alone, and you've been working full-time at a real estate company on the beach?" he asked.

"Yes, sir, that's correct," I said.

"And you got a scholarship to Florida State out of high school two years ago, but you went to the Air Force Academy instead?"

"Yes," I replied, unsure of why he was taking so much interest in my story. He pulled up all my transcripts.

"Young lady, you don't belong here," he said emphatically. "You belong at the main campus in Tallahassee."

I explained that by the time I thought of the FSU option, I had missed the deadline to register for the main campus.

"I'm going to talk to admissions up there, and I'm also going to have them give you the same tuition scholarship we offered you out of high school. I'll connect you with someone to help you find housing and roommates. How's that sound?"

I didn't know why he counseled me like this when I'd just come to register for my fall classes, but I felt a tingle of excitement as I processed everything he'd said. I could now have a more traditional college experience, which I had not had at the other two schools I'd attended. My tuition would be paid for, and I'd be on the main campus, where all the fun was, not to mention full access to all of the majors and courses.

Looking back, I wonder, *Who was that man at the FSU–Panama City campus?* He changed my life in a brief conversation by listening and empathizing. Then like a fairy godfather, he waved his financial aid wand and guided me in a better direction.

Your most important relationships and connections aren't always with people you know. Sometimes they're with people who see something in you, and with compassion, decide to give you a break. If you have influential relationships by virtue of the family you were born into or the career connections you've built over the years, they can really cushion your protective resources with relationships that enhance resilience. But if you don't have those connections yet, just know that sometimes you may make progress through people you don't even know. How you show up and communicate, and the effort you put forth can all influence outcomes through people who don't know you but may still open a door for you, ones you didn't know existed. If you believe that anything is possible, you'll show up in a way that reflects that, which attracts possibilities that might not otherwise unfold. But first, you must be transparent enough to share your story. When you open up to others, you also open yourself to the unexpected miracles that can happen when you connect authentically. Don't pretend or be embarrassed about your situation. Be authentic. In what ways do you need to be more open to sharing your story?

Make the preventive choice to build protective resources and relationships as a way to create more options and make it easier to handle the unexpected. It is a strategy for success, whether you're bringing your vision to fruition or conquering the obstacles to that vision—including growth gaps that can hinder your progress. The good news is that when you are intentional in discovering how you can grow, you can take action to close those gaps.

Coach Yourself

- On a scale of 1 to 10, how well supported do you feel as you seek to attain your vision and goals with ease and energy?
- On a scale of 1 to 10, how well supported do you feel to conquer current or anticipated obstacles and challenges?

- What types of support would enable you to give a higher rating to both questions above?
- In what area do you most need support?
- What would ideal support look like?
- What steps could you take to build and strengthen that support this month and for the rest of this year?
- When will you take those steps?
- What resources do you need to take those steps successfully?

Try This

- ☐ Assess your personal support system.
- ☐ Determine if it needs to be created or nurtured, or if your support system feels complete.
- ☐ If it needs to be created or nurtured, identify one to three actions you will take to strengthen your support system and the timeline to accomplish them.
- ☐ Decide how you will show your appreciation to those people who are a part of your support system.

SAY IT WITH ME:

"I don't go it alone. I welcome and cultivate a strong support system."

RESILIENCE RULE #6

CLOSE YOUR GROWTH GAP

It's not enough to know the steps to take if you don't know how you need to grow in order to take them successfully.

KEY MESSAGES

- Performance goals are your vision; growth goals are the engine.
- A growth mindset builds humility and resilience, but a fixed mindset does the opposite.
- Taking action is the key to growth.

Over 60 percent of second marriages end in divorce.[1]

It wasn't exactly the statistic I wanted to stumble across in the midst of my own divorce, as I privately hoped that one day I'd have a second chance at marriage and maybe even motherhood. Rather than declaring that my future love life was doomed, I got curious. What was different about the 40 percent of second marriages that *lasted*? What did those people do differently that helped them get it right the second time around?

As I searched for answers, I discovered that all their experiences had a similar theme: a commitment to personal growth. The individuals in healthy, lasting second marriages spent a significant amount of energy doing three things.

First, they reflected on how they ended up in a marriage that failed. Were there signs they overlooked? Character flaws they ignored? Insecurities, fears, or nonideal circumstances that guided their decision to enter or end the marriage?

Second, they reflected on how they showed up in their first marriage. What could they have done differently as spouses? How did they contribute to the problems in the marriage? Even in instances where their first spouse was primarily responsible for the issues leading to a divorce, these individuals took responsibility for their own actions, whether they had failed to set boundaries or respond to potential red flags they noticed in the beginning.

Third, they took those lessons and did the work to change before entering another relationship. They decided not simply to *go* through a divorce, but to *grow* through it. The demise of second marriages often stems from the same issues that occurred in first marriages. Personal growth is what makes the difference in eliminating or at least lessening the impact of those issues. This concept is true in every arena of life.

Performance Goals vs. Growth Goals

We are often taught to set goals in a way that can actually lead to failure or guilt. We are encouraged to focus on the steps we need to take to reach a goal or vision. But when we fail to take those steps or are unable to overcome challenges and obstacles in the process, it is easy to become baffled by the problem. We commonly ask ourselves: *What's wrong with me? Why does this goal feel so elusive?* and *Why do I keep getting in the way of or sabotaging my own success?*

After all, you can typically describe the outcomes you want in tangible terms. You know how much you want to weigh, how much money you want to make, what promotion you want to get, what business you want to launch, what relationship you want to nurture. Those are performance goals. You can find many sources that will tell you what steps you should take to achieve them. These goals are easily measurable and concrete, so it is easy to know when the outcome has been attained.

If you and I were chatting over coffee, I might invite you to close your eyes and envision your goals. I'd suggest you picture yourself—six months from now or six years from now—when you've achieved them. I'd ask you to picture what you're wearing, who you're with, what kind of work you're doing, who you're impacting. Being able to see that vision with clarity is important because when you do, you can see how your performance goals—those outcomes that you can easily measure—fit into your vision.

When it comes to getting to your goals and realizing your vision, however, you may be overfocusing on the steps you need to take to get to the goal. Steps are important, of course, but they are irrelevant if your fears, habits, or distractions get in the way of you taking those steps. Most people get stuck and never get to their goals—not because they don't know what steps to take, but because they have not conquered the fears, habits, and distractions that get them stuck when it's time to take those steps.

It's easy to leave out the critical piece: To achieve your desired outcome, you don't just need performance goals; you need *growth goals*. That's the only way to close the *gap between where you are right now and where you really want to be*. The reason for that gap is often invisible or overlooked. It is what you're not seeing that hinders your growth and keeps the gap from closing.

A person struggling in relationships, for example, may never have learned *how* to have a healthy relationship. In fact, they may never have even seen what one looks like if they grew up in a dysfunctional family. For the person who wants to reach a major professional or financial or health goal for the first time, knowing the steps may simply not be enough. A lack of confidence, knowledge, or discipline may be the reason the goal seems out of reach. But if those gaps can be properly *identified*, then they can be closed.

Performance goals are essential, but you need growth goals that power you to achieve them. Did you catch that? *Performance goals are the vision, but growth goals are the engine*. Growth goals are what will get you there. And the job of growth goals is to bridge the gap that's been keeping you stuck.

Where You Get Stuck Is Your Growth Gap

Where is your growth gap?

Perhaps you've set the goal of financial freedom, but you spend emotionally. That's your growth gap. Or maybe you want to write a book, but you procrastinate because a voice in your head tells you that you don't have anything worth saying. When you begin to move toward your performance goal, where do you get stuck? That's your growth gap.

Is it a fear that pops up?

Is it a habit?

Is it a distraction?

The first step to achieving our growth goals is being honest about what our gaps are. For example, I realized I had a growth gap in the area of leadership when I heard John Maxwell speak about the "Law of the Lid" from his book *The 21 Irrefutable Laws of Leadership*.[2] I'd grown my business for years but had goals of going to a higher level. I realized the company could only grow to the level of my leadership. I was the lid! And I needed to rally my resources if I wanted the business to go any higher. I started working on self-development through books, which gave me knowledge, ideas, and wisdom for self-reflection. Then I used the resource of profitability to invest in entrepreneurial and business training. I hired a leadership coach. She shed light on concepts I hadn't considered, such as hiring fractional executives for roles we didn't yet need full-time but whose functions were essential to the growth and systems needed to operate effectively. I asked questions of mentors and those who've "been there, done that." And slowly but surely, I began building a stronger team.

As I write this, the team at The CaPP Institute, the coach training company I founded fifteen years ago, is the best we've ever had. We all feel it. Team members mention it often, saying things like, "We have a great team." "I love everyone I work with." "We are more productive than ever." "I feel so supported." "I feel like I'm growing in my role, and I enjoy that." These are all unsolicited comments. I consider it a fulfilling personal accomplishment to have identified a growth gap and rallied my resources to close it. As a result, I've been able to multiply my purpose and potential in the way I envisioned while creating opportunities for others.

Closing the gap isn't about knowing what steps to take to get to your vision; it's about whether you will actually be able to take those steps when it's time to do so. For example, let's say you have decided to close the growth gap that is keeping you from reaching your fitness goal, so you set your alarm clock for 5:30 a.m. and put your shoes right next to your bed. When the alarm goes off, you have a choice, don't you? One choice you could make is to hit the snooze button. (And your growth gap continues!) But when you decide to close the gap, you make a new choice. You make growth goals that will get you to the finish line. You put one foot on the floor and then the other one. You dress in your workout clothes and brush your teeth. By then you are awake, so you put on your tennis shoes and go work out. Over time, when you keep doing that, you actually change your habits, you change your patterns, and you close the gap. Before you know it, the things that were difficult to do have become your new normal.

IDENTIFY YOUR GROWTH GAP

In my twenties, one of my biggest growth gaps was in the area of finances. I was great at spending money, usually on a credit card. I was an emotional spender. I shopped at expensive stores and financed a nice German car. And then another one! Problem was, I wasn't that great at making money yet. I began reading personal finance books to better understand what I should do to prepare for retirement, buy my own place, and make more money. I was intrigued, and I had a vision. But my financial behavior often led me in the opposite direction of my vision. I had begun to close the growth gap of financial illiteracy by reading and learning from others who succeeded financially. Without recognizing my growth gaps of insecurity and lack of self-control, however, I was unable to actually carry out the steps that my newfound financial literacy taught me. *We cannot meet our growth goals until we close our growth gaps.*

Once I decided to close those growth gaps, I started with a commitment to do no more clothes shopping. I went almost three years without buying anything new unless it was an absolute necessity. Interestingly, that also quelled my appetite for shopping. I hadn't realized it previously, but shopping had been like comfort food to me. But instead of gaining pounds I was gaining debt. My "no clothes shopping" rule was the diet I desperately needed. It was unpleasant, but it got me out of my comfort zone—a place where, at first, I felt vulnerable, but then I got used to it. I faced my fears and what I already knew deep down: that my worth is innate, not material. Next, I decided to set a higher bar for my income. I was in business for myself and adjusted what I offered and how I charged for it. Within two years, I had nearly tripled my income. Closing two growth gaps—self-control and self-worth—gave me the breakthrough I needed to control my spending and increase my income, leading me to climb out of all debt in under three years.

Growth gaps keep us stuck.
Growth goals set us free.

Growth gaps keep us stuck. Growth goals set us free. How far you go is determined by how much you are willing to grow.

I also had a growth gap after going through a divorce, knowing that I still had a desire in my heart for a happy marriage and motherhood. My parents had divorced when I was in college. So I needed to understand what it takes to create and sustain a happy, healthy marriage. I had to learn to trust my instincts and discover how to build a lasting marriage.

Have you ever told yourself, *Because of my past, I don't know how to do this. Therefore, maybe I'm doomed in this area. Maybe I can't have what my heart truly wants.* That's what I was saying to myself, so my growth gap was around relationships. I had a fixed mindset: I had decided that where I was right then was where I would always be stuck.

The light bulb came on for me, though, when I realized that I could change my fixed mindset by closing that growth gap. I had to take a hard look at myself and unpack the impact of growing up in a home where my parents broke up and we didn't talk about it. And so I set some growth goals. I chose to go to therapy so that I could learn how to thrive without falling into codependence, which happens when you acquiesce to dysfunctional behavior as though it is functional and normal. I practiced reflection, taking an honest look at myself. I enlisted a coach. I know that today I would not be a happy wife and mom if I'd refused to overcome my growth gap by pursuing my growth goals.

It's important for you to hear that you don't have to know *why* you have the growth gap in order to make new choices. It is easy to get so caught up in trying to determine what's holding you back that you never stop the behavior that's limiting you. You simply get caught in analysis paralysis. The purpose of identifying the growth gap is not just to figure out what's causing a problem but to develop a plan of action to eliminate or lessen its impact. Do you want to be an expert on the problem or on the solution? Identifying the problem is helpful when it gives you the information you need to come up with the right solution.

Three Categories of Growth Gaps

When we get clear about what our growth gaps are, we can get honest with ourselves and say, "No more! I'm not going to continue to live this way."

Growth is the process of maturing, expanding, or becoming better in some way. A gap is the distance between where you are now and where you need to be to achieve the outcome you want. A growth gap, therefore, is the way in which you need to grow in order to overcome the fear, habit, distraction, or lack of skill that creates the distance between where you are and where you really want to be. Gaps tend to fall into three categories, which we'll break down here.

FEAR

Fear is the most common threat to resilience. There are four core fears—uncertainty, disapproval, failure, and success (which brings increased pressure)—and it's likely that one of these gets you stuck most often. Many people see fear as a stop sign. There is a type of fear that we should heed because it is a legitimate warning to slow down or pause. Fear becomes a growth gap when it keeps you from rising to the occasion. In such situations, you need to find the courage to face the challenge and move forward despite it.

HABITS

We all have had habits that work against our best interests. Whether it's a poor eating habit or a habit of overloading your schedule (hello, anyone else?) or underestimating your abilities, your habits create your reality. Sometimes the growth gap you must close is changing counterproductive habits so you can create a new reality. But first, you must identify the habit or habits that need changing.

DISTRACTIONS

We live in a world filled with distractions. There are the obvious electronic distractions that can keep you from focusing on what matters. And there are the less obvious ones like competing priorities that steal your energy and focus from the challenge in front of you. Whether you are facing increased competition in your business, a challenge in your closest family relationships, or discouragement as you continue a long road to reaching a hard personal goal, it is essential to maintain a focus on what is meaningful over the false urgencies that are so abundant.

When I finally identified my growth gaps—in the areas of my finances and relationships—I was able to create growth goals that helped me get unstuck. And when you identify your growth gaps, you can do the same. Before you can establish those goals, though, you need to get honest about the gaps. Consider the areas below where people commonly have some gaps. Identify the ones where you have room to grow:

- authenticity
- confidence
- consistency
- courage
- discipline
- experience
- focus
- forgiveness
- integrity
- leadership
- knowledge
- mindset
- patience
- perfectionism
- perseverance
- planning
- preparation
- prioritizing
- security
- self-awareness
- self-compassion
- self-forgiveness
- timeliness
- time management

Close the Gaps with a Growth Mindset

Whether it's a fear, a habit, or a distraction, you can choose to close the growth gap. And the way you do that is by developing a growth mindset.

My background is in applied positive psychology, which is just the study of what happens when things go right, when we perform at our highest levels, and when we are happy. Dr. Carol Dweck, a professor of psychology at Stanford University, has made important contributions to this field. For years, Dr. Dweck worked with young students to study how they dealt with failure. One of the ways she did this was by giving students increasingly more difficult puzzles to solve. In particular, she would notice how they responded when they got to the puzzle they could not solve. Many of the students became very discouraged and dejected. But when some students got to the puzzle they could not figure out, they actually seemed to get excited.

They'd rub their hands together. They'd smack their lips. They'd lean in and start trying harder.

She asked those students, "When you got to the puzzle you couldn't figure out, you seemed excited. Why is that?"

And they'd say, "Well, it's a puzzle. I'm about to learn something. There has to be an answer to this. I am about to grow."

Those kids had what she called a growth mindset.[3] They approached challenges with the assumption that their abilities were fluid, so they could get smarter, stronger, and better. Those with a growth mindset don't see big challenges as possibilities that they might fail but rather as opportunities for them to grow. They believe that if they put in the work to learn from an experience and seek resources to help them, they will overcome a challenge. Those with a fixed mindset do not value effort. They tend to rely on the natural abilities they've been praised for, abilities that set them apart and make them special without the extra effort. Often, those abilities have been enough to get them through school and work. But when they face a big enough challenge, refusing to expand and grow means the obstacle will outsize their capacity.

What about you? When faced with a tough challenge, are you more likely to give up or to see the situation as a learning opportunity? Consider the areas in your life where you faced a challenge, got frustrated, and gave up. What if, rather than convincing yourself you weren't good enough to do it, you said,

"I'm not good at this *yet*."

"I could get better."

"I wonder who could help me."

"I wonder what I could read to help solve this."

"I wonder what I could learn."

"I wonder how I could stretch myself."

You can choose to develop a growth mindset by stretching beyond your comfort zone. And when you feel uncomfortable, you can choose to say, "Oh, I'm working to expand my comfort zone; therefore, I am uncomfortable."

The ways you develop a growth mindset are by

- stretching
- learning
- experimenting
- reading
- studying
- coaching

Because these are so critical, I encourage you to be open to experiments. So instead of saying you're going to work out for an hour a day, five days a week, you could say, "This week, I'm going to try working out one hour a day. And let's see how that goes." Then if you successfully work out, notice what enabled you to do so and repeat it. If your experiment doesn't go so well, commit to figuring out what would work better for you. Maybe you choose to commit just thirty minutes a day to exercise. Perhaps you find a buddy who agrees to meet you every morning to take a three-mile walk. Embracing a posture of stretching, learning, experimenting, reading, studying, and coaching are how you close your growth gaps.

A Tool for Your Toolbelt: Take Action

So how do you identify and develop the ability to push through the obstacles that get you stuck on the way to your vision? Much like a physical workout, you've got to take *action*. That is one of the main purposes of coaching. You act and learn from the steps you take. Action builds your mental and emotional muscle:

- Taking action instills confidence.
- Taking action builds your self-concept.
- Taking action is a primary vehicle for learning and growth.
- Taking action helps you build your courage muscles in the face of fear.
- Taking action empowers you to practice what you are not good at so that you can improve.
- Taking action gets you out of your head and into the process of growth.

Your life becomes like a laboratory where you experiment and discover what works and what doesn't. And over time, you develop resilience.

I call this the action-learning process. It is simple and powerful. In fact, if you think of action as a way to learn and grow, that in itself can actually be motivating because the purpose is not to be perfect or get it right, but to learn and get better. Resilience allows room for mistakes in the learning process.

To begin, think about a growth gap you've identified for yourself. Then ask, *What's a simple action I could take to begin growing in this area?*

For example, if you struggle with holding boundaries in a relationship you want to improve, set and communicate a small boundary with your friend or family member. It could be saying no to a recent request that you've been feeling pressured to say yes to even though you don't want to do it. In fact, you could stop and take action right now. Make the call, send the email or text, have the conversation. Once you've communicated with them, reflect on what you learned in the process of taking action. You might learn that it wasn't as hard as you expected or that by writing down what you wanted to say in advance or practicing it in front of a mirror, you were more confident. One simple action will stretch you beyond your comfort zone, and when you succeed at the small steps, you build confidence for the bigger ones.

A Strategy: Three Simple Steps

Three very simple steps can equip you to close your growth gap: set values-driven performance goals, pinpoint your growth gaps, and commit to a personal growth plan.

STEP 1: SET VALUES-DRIVEN PERFORMANCE GOALS

Begin by asking yourself, *What is my performance goal? What is that thing I can measure?* But then ask, *What will this goal give me that I don't already have? What will the money give me? What will the better health give me? What will the relationship give me? What will the promotion give me?* Because sometimes when we ask ourselves that question, we figure out that what it's going to give us isn't even worth it, and it's better to find that out now and drop the goal to free up some space and energy for the things that really do matter. Values must drive your goals; otherwise, once things get difficult you're likely to give up. You'll decide that after all, the goal isn't really all that important to you anyway.

On a scale of 1 to 10, how committed are you to closing any growth gap connected to your performance goal? Are you closer to 10, or are you closer to 1? As you consider this, perhaps you'll discover that the goal is not really rooted in your values. In that case, take the opportunity to go back and reset the goal. Tweak it and make it authentic to you. And if it's not authentic to you, drop it. But if you are clear about why a goal matters, when things get difficult, you can remind yourself how your goal reflects your highest values, making it more likely that you'll persevere.

WHY THIS GOAL?

What's your performance goal?

What will this goal give you that you don't already have?

How does this goal reflect your highest value?

STEP 2: PINPOINT YOUR GROWTH GAPS

How will you need to grow in order to get to the goal? Do you need to become more consistent? Strengthen your leadership skills? Get over some insecurities? What fear, habit, or distraction threatens to keep you from the goal?

WHAT COULD GET IN THE WAY?

What fear, habit, or distraction threatens to keep you from the goal?

How will you need to grow in order to get to the goal?

Spend a bit of time with the list of growth gaps on page 121 and notice which ones are keeping you stuck. If you identify several, that's actually good, because you understand you've got work to do! And you've identified what work needs to be done. When you only set performance goals, you set yourself up for failure, because you're not setting yourself up to determine the engine that's going to get you to that vision. Those are your growth goals!

STEP 3: COMMIT TO A PERSONAL GROWTH PLAN

The plan will differ for all of us, but if you stick to a personal growth plan, you are going to see things change. The bigger the goal, the bigger the commitment needs to be. And little by little, you'll close those growth gaps.

CLOSING THE GAP

- Identify the fear, habit, or distraction that gets you stuck on the way to your goal. (Take a look at the growth gap list on page 121 for help.)
- Pinpoint any support, learning, role models/examples that can help you close your growth gap.
- Decide what action you can experiment with that will begin to build your strength in that growth gap area. This should be something that stretches you beyond your comfort zone.
- Take the action.

You Can Close the Gap

What growth goals will empower you to achieve your most important goal?

I want you to remember that when you close your growth gap, as I did while I was getting out of debt, you're taking the steps to change your behavior. That's why I told myself, *You're banned from the mall until all the debt is paid.* For almost three years, I didn't go to the mall. And you know what? When the three years were over, I didn't really want to go clothes shopping because my values had changed. I didn't need to buy things. I didn't need to impress people who didn't matter that much anyway. I was transformed in the process of closing my growth gap.

So what is your growth gap? I want you to write it down. What growth goals will empower you to achieve your most important goal? What are you going to do differently? Today is a great day for you to figure it out by asking the question, *How do I need to grow?* Be honest about the ways in which you need to grow in order to go where you want to go.

Coach Yourself

- What growth gap do you need to close in order to achieve your meaningful goal?
- How will you know when this growth gap is closed?
- What support, learning, or role model could help you grow in this area?
- What action could you experiment with that will stretch you beyond your comfort zone as you begin to grow in that area? When will you try this?

Try This

- ☐ Start your personal growth plan.
- ☐ Decide how you'll be held accountable.
- ☐ Start growing.
- ☐ Set aside time to reflect on what you learned. (This reflection is like the rest between workouts that helps a muscle recover.)

- ☐ Then identify at least one step per week that will continue to grow that muscle, and reflect on what you are learning and how you are growing.
- ☐ Based on your plan of action, set the date by which you expect to close your growth gap.

SAY IT WITH ME:

"How far I go is determined by how much I am willing to grow."

RESILIENCE RULE #7

DON'T PRETEND, DON'T DEFEND

Why authenticity is a hallmark of resilience and permission to be imperfect is the key to moving forward faster

---

KEY MESSAGES

- Pretending prolongs a problem; admitting it gives you permission to fix it.
- Give yourself permission to be imperfect.
- Use failure to analyze, not penalize.

When you notice a problem, your initial temptation might be to brush it under the rug. Problems and challenges are inconvenient. They mess up your plans. They cloud the picture of how you want things to look. It would be great if they'd just go away. So it's tempting to pretend that they are not there—or to insist that they aren't as big a deal as they are. But that can sabotage success and resilience.

The seventh rule of resilience is this: "Don't pretend, don't defend." It is a mantra to remind you to muster the courage to face reality. After all, you can't conquer what you aren't willing to confront. What you ignore becomes the blind spot that can undermine your resilience.

Let me explain. "Don't pretend" is the first half of this rule because you can fix a problem only if you first admit there is one! If you act as if everything is okay when it isn't, resilience is improbable, if not impossible. "Don't defend" is the second half of this rule because sometimes your own decisions or behavior land you in a bad place.

Perhaps you made a mistake. It happens, but maybe you'd rather pretend it didn't. And that can lead to defensiveness about needed changes that could empower you to make amends, learn a lesson, or bounce back. So don't pretend things are okay that are not, and don't defend imperfections, mistakes, or poor choices. Be brave enough to admit what is true. Be authentic. Then take responsibility for addressing the issue so it doesn't persist.

What you ignore becomes the blind spot that can undermine your resilience.

The Problem with Pretending

You can close your eyes and pretend you don't see something. Or you can keep your eyes open and look realistically at the truth, no matter how ugly, inconvenient, or unwanted it may seem. Being honest is like turning on a light switch. You can make the resilient choice to face a challenge and decide what you want to do in light of it. This allows you to move from a passive stance to a proactive one. It empowers you to take responsibility for what is within your control. The truth will set you free, but only when you are honest enough to face it.

What are some examples of pretending that sabotage your resilience?

- insisting you're okay when you are not
- denying reality
- protesting that you don't need help when you do
- hiding or downplaying an issue to avoid talking about it
- saying things you don't mean
- avoiding uncomfortable feelings
- focusing on "fitting in" rather than just being yourself

Pretending is a coping mechanism. When dealing with a challenge, our natural reaction may be to downplay, or even deny, the reality of the situation. We might not even notice we're doing it, but ignoring or trying to minimize reality gives us the illusion of control and temporarily eases feelings of fear and vulnerability. We tiptoe around issues or minimize them. We deny we need to make a change. And too often, we allow fear to make our decisions and dictate our actions.

USE MISTAKES TO ANALYZE, NOT PENALIZE

In addition to allowing the consequences of mistakes to fester, ignoring problems makes it much harder to learn from our failures and improve our resilience. An intriguing example of the power of truth-telling comes from the aviation industry. At the time I wrote these words, the largest commercial airlines in the United States had gone over fifteen years without even one fatal crash due to airline pilot error.[1] That means they'd safely carried more than 10 billion passengers and made over 100 million flights soaring 30,000 feet over land and sea in pressurized metal tubes. As far back as the 1960s, flying was considered one of the safest ways to travel. Back then, there was about one death per 350,000 passengers. Today, though, there is one death per 13.7 million passengers.[2] That makes flying safer than walking across the street!

My husband, Jeff, a former airline captain who flew commercially for twenty years, now trains professional pilots. He often talks about changes in the industry that explain why flying has become so much safer. His reputation for ensuring the airplanes he flew were safe and well-maintained caught the attention of the safety chairman for his pilot union, who asked Jeff to become the chief accident investigator and help the union in their quest to get their airline to participate in a new Federal Aviation Administration (FAA) program that empowered pilots to self-report mistakes in flight without retribution.

The FAA's Aviation Safety Action Program (ASAP) encourages employees "to voluntarily report safety issues even though they may involve an alleged violation of . . . Federal Regulations."[3] Prior to the advent of the program, pilots were very hesitant to reveal their mistakes because it often proved detrimental to their careers. Mistakes could potentially result in a range of consequences, from a letter of warning in their personnel file or a fine, to the suspension or revocation of their pilot's license, which could result in a demotion or end their career. As a result, there was a clear incentive to pretend mistakes had not happened and keep quiet.

It also meant that airlines had little insight into the type or frequency of undetected mistakes that could turn into accidents. What were the patterns? Where were the blind spots? What should be done to prevent the next serious accident? Without honesty about mistakes, there was no way to accurately come up with answers—and the cost was devastating. Until recently, commercial airline accidents were more frequent and deadly.

In 1996, the year before ASAP launched, 355 people died in domestic airline accidents in the United States.[4] Within a decade, the fatal accident rate dropped by 65 percent.[5] And the fatal accident rate has declined even further since then. Improvements in technology deserve some credit for the decline, but another major factor is the commitment to improving safety by creating an environment where pilots can be transparent and truthfully self-report their errors.

ASAP was revolutionary when it was launched. The idea was that rather than penalizing mistakes, the industry could analyze them. That analysis could then be used to improve safety. The old system focused on analyzing accidents after they occurred. The central theme of the new system is to prevent accidents in the first place by learning from the mistakes pilots self-report. Some of these errors offered opportunities to improve procedures and technology that would make the mistake obsolete. Other errors alerted airlines to areas in which more training was needed; in fact, some self-reports became case studies used in training. Without the information provided through self-reports, such improvements would have been completely missed, making it likely the mistakes would occur again, leading to crashes, injuries, and lost lives. The program dramatically impacts the bottom line, too, as a crash of a single jumbo jet can lead to financial losses of about $1 billion, according to estimates.[6]

When it was launched, ASAP was a controversial idea because

it relied on pilots admitting mistakes, and there was skepticism that they would. Airlines would need to agree that pilots wouldn't be punished for their errors. They might be sent for more training, but they weren't going to lose their jobs and livelihood. And pilots would need to trust their airlines with this new approach. Over time, pilots observed that the ASAP program was not punitive. The ASAP program illustrates the power of the first pillar of resilience, an adaptive skill that resulted in a complete shift in how the aviation industry thought about, reacted to, and made decisions that affected its most important challenge: keeping people safe while traveling.

Consequently, the culture and relationships changed, not just between the airlines and pilots, but between airline competitors. Airlines had to be convinced to share their data so it could be studied for the greater good of the industry. This cultural shift reflects the strengthening that can come from the second pillar of resilience, the protective resource of strong relationships and a willingness to share information. The third pillar of resilience, preventive measures, has been strengthened as the ASAP program gives airlines life-saving insight into potential future problems and the ability to fix those problems before they turn into fatal accidents. And now other industries, such as health care, manufacturing, and artificial intelligence are looking to implement this approach.

ALLOW HONESTY TO POINT YOU TO THE REAL PROBLEMS

One of the lessons we can glean from the airline industry's ASAP program is the power of using mistakes and failures as learning tools, a hallmark of resilience. This can happen only when you admit to mistakes. Many motivators, from negative consequences to shame or embarrassment, can entice you to avoid telling yourself the truth. But the moment you embrace honesty, you can ask, *What is the message in this for me?* Whatever it is, you can use it to get better, stronger, and wiser. Analyze mistakes and failures—not so you can penalize yourself or beat yourself up, but so you can fix them, grow from them, or prevent future problems.

HONESTY (WITH YOURSELF) IS THE BEST POLICY

Think about an area of your life where you need to be resilient right now—whether your work, relationships, physical health, and even your emotional, mental, or spiritual health. What would it look like to be truthful about your situation? Coach yourself with these questions:

- What am I most afraid to admit about the situation?
- What am I *not* saying about the situation?
- In what way(s) am I minimizing or denying reality?
- What insecurities or fears are driving me to keep this quiet?

Resilience requires an unrelenting embrace of the truth. But that often comes with consequences. So there is an incentive either to ignore or even pretend you don't know it. If you make a mistake at work, covering it up or quietly patching up the problem could ensure you still get that promotion or maintain a high level of respect from your colleagues. In a worst-case scenario, it might save your job or keep a customer from getting you fired. However, ignoring or denying the truth keeps you from addressing, and even reconciling, bigger underlying problems. It keeps you from putting in place the kinds of preventive measures that could make you much more successful and resilient in the future. And it steals your integrity.

How Are You Pretending?

The rule "Don't pretend, don't defend" is rooted in the power of authenticity, honesty, and humility. To be resilient, you must first acknowledge the reality of your situation. The sooner you accept that there is a problem to address, the better position you are in to solve it—or at least reduce its negative impact.

Resilience is hard work. And it starts with getting honest.

WHY ADMITTING IT'S HARD MAKES YOU STRONGER

Research shows that just naming the thing that is creating stress lowers your stress level by reducing cortisol levels in your body.[7] Try it right now. Take a slow, deep breath. Maybe even try another research-based tip: stroke your arm gently and think about the challenge that stresses you these days.[8] Then say to yourself, *This challenge is hard. I am resilient, but it's taking extra energy to push through it.* Simple words such as this trigger a physiological response. And gentle, affirming touch releases dopamine and other feel-good chemicals that lower stress.

It is a myth that to be strong, you must be fearless and let nothing bother you. This idea is the epitome of pretending. After all, everyone feels fear. Insisting stressors are not troubling you requires you to bury real feelings; as a result, you cannot be authentic. Fear is a natural human response to real and perceived threats in your environment. Fear can be good too. There are many things you should indeed be afraid of. Legitimate threats abound. Fear is a warning system that gives you information like "Be careful," "Prepare for what's coming," "Don't go there," or "Don't do that."

Dealing with fear activates your body's fight-or-flight response. When it senses danger, your amygdala—the part of the brain that processes emotions—sends signals that increase your blood pressure and cortisol levels, getting you ready to fight or flee. While we think of these as responses to physical stress, our bodies react in a similar way even when the threat is emotional.

Simply admitting that something is hard or stressful is an act of self-compassion. Self-compassion has a physiological effect by reducing cortisol levels and increasing feel-good chemicals such as oxytocin, according to Dr. Kristin Neff, a researcher and professor at the University of Texas at Austin and author of *Self-Compassion*. This has a soothing effect that makes you more resilient by decreasing your stress level.[9]

Whether the stressor is a deadline you've missed, a mistake you've made at work, or an unwanted personal challenge, being honest enough to acknowledge that what you're pushing through is hard will actually make you stronger.

You know that first little tickle in your throat that tells you you're about to come down with a cold? You can pretend you don't feel the tickle. You can tell yourself it's nothing. "The weather is changing! It's allergies! I'm fine!" you insist. But you can only ignore it for so long before the symptoms become too obvious to ignore. Even if you deny them, others will notice. "You sound stuffy," they'll say. "Oh my goodness, that cough sounds awful! Have you gone to the doctor?" Eventually, the reality of your symptoms interferes with your ability to keep going. The sooner you address the inconvenient truth, the sooner you can address the symptoms and the faster you can bounce back. The same is true with any challenge. Acting like a problem isn't a problem multiplies its impact.

Authenticity Is a Hallmark of Resilience

Authenticity, the degree to which your actions align with your values and beliefs, is a hallmark of resilience. That's because your ability to be resilient is directly correlated with your ability to think accurately about yourself and the world around you. A sober relationship with reality empowers you to

- address challenges faster
- find solutions sooner
- minimize and even prevent future challenges
- preserve and increase energy and strength
- persevere more effectively

Sometimes authenticity doesn't come easily though. If being yourself and acknowledging your vulnerabilities feel too threatening, it can seem much easier to pretend and present a front that allows you to feel safer, even if it creates other issues you'll have to deal with later.

Authenticity, according to Czech researchers, "expresses the degree of a person's self-identity" as well as the connection between their behavior and their self-concept.[10] Our perceptions of who we are and what we are capable of go to the core of our self-perception. Even without consciously realizing it, we can go to extremes to protect that image of ourselves. That's because, when reality doesn't line up with how we see ourselves, the foundation of who we think we are and who we want to be is shaken.

IS THE TRUE YOU SHOWING?

Authenticity means ensuring that your coworkers, family, and friends are seeing the true you.

- Are you being your true self? How do you know?
- Can others trust that what you do and say reflects what you actually think and believe? What is the evidence of this?

For example, you likely want to see yourself as capable and competent at work. As a result, you may want to reject anything that challenges that self-concept. You may avoid opportunities that stretch you too much, even though they could be advantageous long-term, because you don't want to feel or be seen as incapable or incompetent. You may decline assistance even though you need it because receiving help forces you to acknowledge a weakness or insecurity. This can happen when you have a fixed mindset rather than a growth mindset. If you are more interested in maintaining the status quo than in growing, when you bump against hard challenges you may conclude, *I must not be as smart as I thought.* As a result, you sabotage your own success.

In the area of finances, you may see yourself as someone who earns more than you do, has no debt, and always negotiates for the best terms of a deal. So facing the mountain of debt you've created or figuring out how to stop underearning and boost your income may mess with your self-concept. As a result, you may pretend things aren't as bad as they actually are. The decision to live in denial isn't always a conscious one, but it is always a detrimental one. That's because it keeps you from seeing the challenge realistically so you can solve it. This piles on more challenges.

In my twenties, I was just like that—in debt but continuing to spend. I didn't even want to add up my debt because I didn't want to know just how much I owed! I became resilient to move through that challenge the moment I got honest and embraced authenticity.

That caused me to see soberly and stop connecting my self-worth with my net worth. It was hard! I felt vulnerable, afraid I'd be judged or rejected if I didn't appear to be financially successful through the things I bought. It was faulty thinking since outward appearances don't tell you much about someone's financial status. But through self-coaching and authentic reflection, I changed my entire mindset, which led to a transformation in my emotional, spiritual, and financial well-being.

My client Cameron was a compassionate executive whose marketing director, John, was struggling to meet expectations. John had strong family connections in the company that had served as a protective resource to help him navigate challenges. In this case, rather than firing John, Cameron worked with human resources to hire a slightly overqualified assistant for him. Cameron and the HR manager strategized that the new assistant would support John in reaching his goals. One way of looking at the assistant was as another protective resource who could help John meet expectations—and improve his performance. But John's insecurities upended that idea. Instead of seeing her as someone who could help him, John felt threatened by the educational level of this new employee and refused to fully utilize her skill set for fear she would make him look bad. Rather than recognizing that his skill set was weak in a couple of areas, he sabotaged his own success by refusing to leverage the strengths of his new team member. Seeing little improvement in John's performance in the months that followed, Cameron and her fellow executives decided the best option was to let John go. His rejection of help and lack of awareness of his weaknesses were issues they could no longer tolerate.

John could have kept his job by facing the truth about his shortcomings and doing something about them, rather than allowing them to become insecurities that he chose to deny or defend. Deep down, John knew he was falling short, but admitting that made him feel like he never should have landed the job in the first place. He also knew that he'd been given an advantage over other candidates because of his family connections, but that benefit had been squandered by his poor performance too. Now he was out of work and needed to look for another job. If he had faced reality, working to improve in the areas where his boss had given him negative feedback and tapping into the strengths of his assistant, Cameron says she would have continued to work with John. "He wasn't performing, and he refused to see how his lack of performance was a drag on everyone," she reflected. "He didn't have the emotional maturity to be honest and humble so he could address the problems. If he had been, we could have worked through it."

An inability to be honest about realities has a ripple effect. In John's case, openness to negative but constructive feedback would have allowed him to work on improving in areas where the company said he was struggling. And if he didn't want to improve, he would have recognized what was coming and planned for a job change. In either case, he would have shown resilience under the circumstances. Instead, John told himself that the feedback he'd been given was inaccurate and that the situation wasn't that bad, even though Cameron made clear that changes were coming if there was no improvement. His adaptive skills were lacking, and his entire perspective was rooted in blame and defensiveness. He did not take ownership or responsibility for his behavior. Because he would not confront reality, his employer didn't see him as coachable or teachable, and decided to hit the reset button on the marketing position.

What's Your Goal? What's the Obstacle?

I don't know what goals are a part of your vision, but I bet there are some dreams you'd love to see unfold. What are they? Just as importantly, what obstacles will you need to push through to make them reality? Whatever the obstacles, the first step to overcoming them is seeing them and then finding a way to push through them, move around them, or eliminate them altogether. Don't pretend they are not there. Don't minimize their significance. Be honest with yourself. Take a deep breath and face them head-on.

Here are some simple, wise ways to implement the "Don't pretend" rule and embrace authenticity, humility, and truth in your work and relationships.

1. **Think accurately, not just positively.** The most resilient people aren't just positive thinkers. They recognize that there are things that can go wrong, risks they need to account for, and very real challenges to address.

   If your only strategy is to stay positive, you will positively fail. It's more about what you choose to be positive about. Even as you maintain a positive attitude, recognize the reality of obstacles and challenges with a view to finding a way around those challenges.

2. **Reject the myth of fearlessness.** One of the most insidious ideas about success is that successful people are fearless. That's a myth. And it basically excuses us from pushing past fear. If people succeed because they are free of fear, then if you feel fear, you have an excuse to stop moving forward, right? It's a ridiculous notion. Everyone feels fear. The most successful people learn to have courage in the face of their fear. So they move forward afraid.

   Acknowledge what you are afraid of. Name it. Then decide to do what you need to do even though you feel afraid. Progress and fear can coexist. In fact, they must if you are to be resilient.

3. **Be humble.** Humility makes resilience so much easier. When your self-concept accepts your imperfections, there is nothing to hide. You know you're not perfect. Your goal is to learn and grow so you can become better, wiser, and stronger. When you

make a mistake, you acknowledge it. And this makes you real. It makes you authentic. It makes you coachable.

4. **Admit when you need help.** Once you embrace humility and authenticity, it's easier to accept help. You don't see it as a flaw. Instead, it is evidence of your humanity and acceptance that those who are most resilient are those who do not go it alone. If you've bought into the idea that somehow needing help means you are weak, and weakness means you are less valuable, capable, or intelligent, let that idea go. When you change how you interpret the meaning of help, you change how it makes you feel to ask for and receive it.

   Our culture celebrates independence to a fault. A better goal is interdependence. We don't want to be dependent on others for all things. After all, we need to be responsible. However, if we are interdependent, we recognize that strong relationships are built when we help others and allow others to help us, each using our strengths for the benefit of the greater good.

5. **Communicate what's okay and what's not okay.** Speak up and set clear boundaries. When you do, people don't have to guess about what's acceptable to you. You tell them. When they cross a boundary, you address it and take steps to protect it when needed. This alone will change your life. Setting boundaries is a preventive choice in the three-pillar resilience framework because it stops many problems before they start.

6. **Tell the truth.** One of the most common ways I've helped clients with challenging conversations over the years is to simply ask them, "What makes this hard to bring up?" Inevitably, the client shares thoughts such as "I am anxious about having the conversation," "I don't want them to get upset, stop talking to me, or misconstrue what I am saying," or "I care about this person, but I can't keep dealing with this issue." My response as a coach? "Why don't you say *to them* what you just said to me?"

I offer the same advice to you. Just be up front. Maybe it's a relationship that is long overdue for a hard conversation, an issue it's time to finally solve, or perhaps a habit that is having a negative impact. Authenticity means telling the truth, not just in the big things, but in the small ones too.

7. **Compliment what you admire.** Rather than being intimidated by the strengths, capabilities, or accomplishments of others, acknowledge them. Someone else being good at something doesn't diminish your strengths. Authentic people don't withhold genuine compliments and appreciation for the value others bring. Their authentic expressions of gratitude and awe build trust and connection in their relationships, which ultimately strengthens relationship bonds and resilience.

8. **Slow down when you see a yellow flag.** Ever have that gut feeling that something is off, only to ignore it and then later regret that you did? It might not be a red flag, but it's definitely a yellow one. Don't pretend you didn't see what you saw because it's inconvenient or will require you to step outside of your comfort zone to deal with it. When you are honest with yourself, you don't brush off little warning signs. Slow down. Pay attention. Reflect on whether what you've observed is a warning sign or just an isolated instance.

9. **Be consistent.** Authenticity means showing up in the same way consistently. Your values and actions should remain the same regardless of who you are with or who might notice. Consistency is an important component of integrity. And integrity makes you stronger by reducing the problems and strife that can emerge when it's lacking. Do what's right day after day.

10. **Acknowledge your feelings.** Feelings don't mean you are weak. They simply mean you are human. One of the most powerful

things you can do is name your feelings. When an emotion arises, especially an uncomfortable one, label it: "That's fear." "That's guilt." "That's jealousy." By acknowledging the feeling, you also create an interruption that can help you think before acting on the emotion. In an article for *The New York Times*, Tony Schwartz observes, "Noticing and naming emotions gives us the chance to take a step back and make choices about what to do with them."[11] But stuffing feelings down and pretending they aren't there causes them to come out in other unhealthy and self-sabotaging ways.

> **THE POWER OF ACTING "AS IF"**
>
> Coach yourself with this question:
>
> How would I act if
>
> I had the courage to . . .
>
> I had the strength to . . .
>
> I was confident that . . .
>
> I had the faith to . . .
>
> In other words, imagine yourself acting as if you already are what you need to be to respond with resilience in the situation. By doing so, you shift your mindset from one of doubt, fear, or hesitation to seeing yourself as a stronger, better, wiser version—and then acting *as if* that is who you are. Unlike pretending and defending, acting *as if* elevates your thinking by helping you step into the authentic vision of who you want to be.

11. **Act "as if."** One popular piece of advice is to "fake it till you make it." While this sounds counter to authenticity, there is one little bit of truth to this idea. When you have doubts about your ability to handle a challenge, researchers suggest a technique called "acting 'as if.'"[12] It's similar to pretending, but it's really a way of focusing on embodying the traits you aspire to. You imagine what you would do *if* you were the person you want to be. This simply means acting as if you have the strength to do what you set out to do. You show up in the situation *as if* you were resilient, disciplined, or courageous. It creates a powerful shift in mindset.

What Are You Defending?

What about when you need resilience, not because of something beyond your control, but because of something you did? The second part of Resilience Rule #7 is "don't defend," which goes a step beyond acknowledging a problem. It means having the humility and courage to face the truth about your own mistakes and shortcomings so you can repair the damage to relationships and create the healing that will empower you to move forward. It means not rationalizing poor choices and decisions, but admitting them, atoning for them, and learning from them.

Defending goes a step beyond pretending. Pretending is what you do with yourself, denying reality in order to cope with your own emotions, fears, and self-concept. When our own mistakes and poor choices lead to a reality that conflicts with our idea of who we are, it can be tempting to defend that self-concept by not acknowledging or confronting those wrong or unwise actions. Defending insists that others also play along with our denial of reality.

If you pretend long enough, eventually you have to defend. It reminds me of a series of three small driving accidents about nine months after I'd barely passed my driver's test. My car was a $400 "snow car" my dad had bought from a coworker. If you grew up or live in a place where it snows a lot, it's nice to have a car you don't mind getting dinged in the snow. "Flo," as I named her for her fluorescent yellow color, was a Volkswagen Rabbit stick shift with faux sheepskin seat covers.

The first incident occurred as I was giving a friend's younger brother a ride home from school. I slid across a sheet of ice while rounding a corner, hitting the curb with a loud thud, and landing in the crunchy, snow-covered grass. I managed to slowly drive us back to the school as one of the tires made a persistent and rhythmic clunking noise with every rotation. Turns out I'd bent the axle. A mechanic fixed it, or so we thought. Eight months later, the engine mount broke. Apparently, I'd also cracked that when I hit the curb, and it eventually gave way to the engine's weight. On another occasion, I bumped the front of the garage while parking, creating a dent in the drywall and a crack in the cement baseboard. I hoped no one would notice, and when they did, I pretended I had no idea how it happened.

The third mishap was the most egregious, though. One day after school, I backed out of the garage and down our short driveway, which was lined with small pencil shrubs. For a reason I can only attribute to my novice driving skills, I didn't back straight down the driveway. Nope. I curved a little to the left and split two small bushes right down the middle! I am embarrassed to admit that not only did I *pretend* I didn't do it, but I also made up an elaborate story to *defend* myself: "You see, I was sitting at the dining room table doing homework when I heard wheels screeching on the pavement outside," I explained to my mother. "I looked out the window and a car was taking off directly from our driveway and speeding down the street! I ran outside, and that's when I noticed they'd run over our bushes!"

I know, not my best moment. I told an outright lie rather than admitting I accidentally ran over the bushes. My mom was skeptical but seemed to buy it—that is, until she mentioned it to one of her friends over the phone. Her friend responded, "Lee, come on! That makes no sense!" But of course, not only had I run over the bushes, I had lied about doing it as well.

If I had fessed up, I might have had to pay for new bushes, but if I was caught lying—well, that consequence would be much worse. So I *defended* my story. And the consequence of that was deeper. It meant my word couldn't always be trusted. Just writing that last sentence still stings. Who wants to be thought of as untrustworthy? But pretending all is well when it isn't eventually leads to defending your stance to others. And that can take a toll on your relationships, which are key to solving challenges and maintaining your well-being. By defending after pretending, you create more problems than you started with.

Give Yourself Permission to Be Imperfect

We all make mistakes. We even do things we shouldn't and need a second chance. When that happens, the humility to acknowledge our imperfections gives us resilience. "Don't defend" is about *accepting* who you are and where you are, without your ego jumping in to make you look good at the expense of the truth or avoiding hard conversations and facing consequences. It is an adaptive skill because it relates to how you think, adapt, and react to challenges.

Authentic people are honest—with themselves and others. But that's not always convenient. If you are in denial about the reality of a situation, you will defend choices and decisions that line up with your denial. Here are some examples:

- The leader who is a terrible communicator and blames the team for misunderstanding instructions will not only alienate team members, but will also cause repeated problems on the way to a goal. Those issues will not be resolved until the leader takes an honest look within or the leader is no longer in the role.

- The person who is passive-aggressive instead of direct will defend rudeness or questionable comments and create distrust and resentment in relationships, eventually losing or damaging them beyond repair.

- The company that disregards customer complaints and employee insights, instead choosing to defend poor practices, frustrating customers and/or employees, will eventually take a hit to their bottom line.

- The parent who never apologizes when they are wrong and makes excuses whenever they do the same things they fuss at their children about—using a "do as I say, not as I do" approach—causes their children to feel resentment and frustration.

Pay Attention to the Warning Signs

The seventh rule of resilience doesn't just ask you not to pretend but also advises, "Don't defend."

Refusing to defend mistakes, even small ones, can prevent bigger issues down the road. Those solo accidents I had at sixteen were a warning sign I didn't heed. The summer after my first year of college, I was hit by a pickup truck that ran a red light and ran into my driver's side at a major intersection. I blacked out and don't remember much about the accident. Soon after that, I began having major problems with my back that have continued. For once, the accident was not my fault. It was caused by a teenage driver who sped past a police car that was sitting at the red light. His light had been red long enough for the left-turn arrow in front of me to run through a cycle. When our traffic light finally turned green, the cars in the two lanes to my left noticed the oncoming truck barreling through the intersection and stayed put. I didn't see it, however. I hadn't looked to my left or right before pushing on the gas. Taking off without making sure the coast was clear was a novice's driving mistake.

If my parents and I had paid attention to the warning signs before that accident, we might have acknowledged that I needed driving lessons. From a resilience perspective, driver's education is a preventive measure. I had never taken driver's ed because I was younger than my high school friends, and I didn't want to take it on my own after them. I decided to opt out of it and study on my own instead. The multiple mishaps were a warning sign about my questionable driving skills back then and a precursor to the accident I wish had never happened.

Humility, authenticity, and honesty are all adaptive approaches that keep you from defending mistakes and failures. Humility about your mistakes and shortcomings can empower you to address issues and save yourself more trouble in the future, making it possible for you to take preventive measures to fix issues rather than defend and ignore them. Ask yourself, *How would responding with humility, authenticity, and honesty to a challenge I face enable me to navigate it more effectively?* Here are some practical ways to stop defending yourself.

1. **Listen for the grain of truth.** Sometimes the feedback we get isn't constructive criticism, but rather destructive criticism. The resilient response is to take a breath and honestly ask yourself if there is a grain of truth in what has been said. Even if there is just 10 percent of truth in the criticism, use that information to get better.

2. **Be coachable.** Be open to growing and trying new ways of doing things. You may find that the challenge in front of you is an opportunity to stretch and improve in some way.

3. **Learn from others.** The wisdom of humility is accepting that you can't possibly know everything. There is something to learn from others; sometimes even from those who don't have as much experience as you. They still have a perspective you need to hear.

4. **Acknowledge your own mistakes and poor choices.** We all make blunders and errors in judgment we'd rather undo. Learn from the situation and change your future behavior. When you are humble about errors and bad choices, you are also more empathetic and compassionate with others, thereby strengthening relationships that help you forge solutions authentically.

5. **Replace blame with responsibility.** A telltale sign of defensiveness is blame, which we use to try to self-protect and escape guilt. Take responsibility for your part in a problem, even if it is small. If you are a leader in any capacity, take responsibility for what you could have done better to prevent the situation.

6. **Do not withhold an apology when you are wrong or cause harm.** When you're wrong, do what you can to right the situation. Apologize. Accept responsibility. Fix the problem if possible, or at least help ease difficulties that were created by what you did.

7. **Listen to the other point of view.** Humility enables us to respect others' opinions and ways of doing things. Instead of defending your point of view, allowing another person to be heard often opens the door to resolution of conflict. That's partly because positive interactions make it easier to communicate and collaborate. And feeling heard produces positive emotions in a relationship, even when the two parties do not agree.

What unwanted realities are you dealing with? What opportunities and blessings also come with the stress you must manage? You have it in you to navigate your toughest challenges, and you'll do so more quickly and easily if you don't pretend things are okay when they aren't or defend poor choices or behaviors.

Responding in these ways can feel vulnerable, but they're worth it. If you are willing to be uncomfortable, your comfort zone and your capacity to push through challenges will expand. Don't pretend and don't defend. You'll be better, wiser, and stronger for it.

Coach Yourself

- What is one situation or mistake that you'd like to pretend didn't exist?
- What are you denying, resisting, or pretending is true that really isn't?
- What are you *not* saying?
- As you consider any difficult feedback you've received recently, what is the grain of truth you hate to admit?

- ▶ What would it look like to accept the reality of the challenge?
- ▶ What would be different if you stopped pretending?
- ▶ What would be different if you chose not to be defensive?
- ▶ In what areas do you need to give yourself permission to be imperfect?
- ▶ If you exercised humility in that previous situation you wish did not exist, what would shift for the better?
- ▶ If you exercised the courage to be authentic, what could shift for the better?

Try This

- ☐ Identify what you are resisting, denying, or avoiding.
- ☐ Decide to admit the problem so you can begin to address it.
- ☐ If there is an area where you have been defensive, choose humility and courage so you can take responsibility, learn, and repair any damage that has been done.

SAY IT WITH ME:

*"When I admit the problem,
I can fix the problem."*

RESILIENCE RULE #8

FIND THE OPPORTUNITY IN THE CHALLENGE

Why you should embrace optimism (most of the time) if you want to find the gifts your situation is offering you

---

KEY MESSAGES

- Intentionally embrace a specific type of optimism that predicts success and resilience.
- Anticipate and cultivate post-traumatic growth.
- "Constructive interpretations" can transform your challenges into opportunities.

About a year after he opened a McDonald's franchise in Sierra Vista, Arizona, the owner realized he was losing out on a lucrative source of income: soldiers from the nearby Fort Huachuca army base. A long-standing rule prohibited them from getting out of their vehicles when wearing their fatigues off base.

McDonald's franchises nationwide had been around for two decades at that point, and not one of them had a drive-through window. The franchisee in Sierra Vista was desperate to boost sales, so he got creative and turned the challenge into an opportunity that changed McDonald's nationwide. He knocked a hole in the wall and installed a window, and on January 24, 1975, the first McDonald's drive-through was born. Today, the drive-through window is synonymous with McDonald's, and 70 percent of their sales nationwide come from those orders.[1]

This next rule opens the door for creativity and hope, adaptive skills that can help you navigate challenges in surprisingly agile and effective ways. The rule is this: "Find the opportunity in the challenge."

When faced with an obstacle, it can be tempting to become frustrated by overfocusing on the problem. One of the most powerful questions to coach yourself with is this: *What's the opportunity in this challenge?* There is often a message in the midst of the mess, but when you refuse to look for it, you can miss out. The problem doesn't have to be good in order for something good to come of it. If you intentionally look at your challenge from a different perspective, you can interpret the difficulty in a way that inspires you to make resilient choices about how to react. Our responses are determined by how we choose to think.

With a shift in perspective, it becomes easier to see the opportunity offered to you in the midst of a challenge. You might not have wanted things to go the way they have, but since they did, ask yourself, *How do I want to show up? What do I want to do? What is the opportunity in this?* Opportunity can look like

- **Something new.** Is there a chance to do something you haven't done before?
- **Lessons.** What lesson(s) can you learn from this challenge? What wisdom can you glean?
- **Start over/reset.** The end of something often makes room for the beginning of something else—something good, something better, perhaps even a chance to start over that otherwise wouldn't exist.
- **Expanded comfort zone.** Maybe what you really need is courage, and this is a chance to develop it. When you learn to get comfortable with being uncomfortable, you're in a position to grow.
- **Gratitude.** Contentment begins with thankfulness. Perhaps your opportunity is very simple—a profound act of gratitude and a chance to focus on what you have, not what you don't.

- **A decision.** When things don't go as planned, you often have to make decisions you would not need to make otherwise. Sometimes those decisions become the pivotal points that can change your life for the better.

Adopt Constructive Interpretations

When it comes to being resilient, it's not what happens that matters most. The challenge alone does not determine how resilient we'll become. Some people are permanently knocked down by challenges that others overcome every day. The element that most determines how effectively someone will approach a challenge is how they interpret it. This is a part of how they think, an adaptive skill that can strengthen their resilience.

Constructive interpretations are a way of reframing negative situations so that you're inspired to move forward and become more resilient. Simple questions such as "What might be another way to look at this challenge?" or "What can I learn from this experience to enhance future opportunities?" or "What does this give me a chance to try or do that I wouldn't have before?" can shift your mindset.

For example, two people can be laid off from the same company and interpret the situation in entirely different ways. Their interpretation will dictate how they view the problem, what they say to themselves about the future, and whether or not they take action, as well as what actions they choose to take. Notice the difference in the way Adam and Vivian, who worked in public relations at the same company, responded to a layoff.

Although Adam hadn't been expecting to be let go, he didn't take it personally. After the company missed its revenue goals for several quarters without announcing any planned launches or remedies to increase revenue or cut expenses, he had wondered if there would be layoffs. He knew such plans might not be publicly announced but figured the public relations department might be at risk. He hoped his position wouldn't be cut. Unfortunately, it was. Or maybe, just maybe, it could turn out to be a stroke of good fortune.

Adam quickly saw it as an opportunity and decided to pursue something he had wanted to pursue for a long time. He had been quietly working on a business in his spare time and dreamed of finally branching out on his own. He knew his severance package would last for only about six months, so he had to work quickly if he was going to make a go of the business full-time. After four months, Adam had made progress, but not enough to meet his financial goals. So he began interviewing for positions and landed a job with a competitor of his former employer's. Though he now earned more than he had when he was laid off, he didn't give up on his business goal. After two years, he made the entrepreneurial leap he'd been dreaming about.

His coworker and counterpart, Vivian, was devastated by the layoff. Though Adam had also been a solid member of the team, Vivian's skill set and performance were actually better than his. She often downplayed her skills and underestimated her value to the team. She was perplexed by Adam's optimism and willingness to see the layoff as anything but the insult that it was. During her eight years at the company, Vivian had always received stellar performance reviews, but the layoff caused her to question her worth and value.

Vivian saw her layoff as a personal failure that indicated she didn't measure up. It hurt her confidence. Like Adam, she had started a part-time business, but she viewed it as just a hobby and didn't consider going into business for herself.

She began to doubt she could convince another company to hire her, which made her second-guess whether to apply for positions that met her qualifications. She was slow to reach out to her connections, embarrassed by the idea of being out of work and needing to rely on others to help her find a new job. To cope, she subconsciously told herself she didn't really need a job that badly. This made her feel less desperate. It also gave her an excuse to procrastinate. Eventually, when she realized she was about to run out of money, Vivian hastily took a position she didn't want.

Adam and Vivian faced the same challenge with the same company at the same time, but they interpreted the situation differently.

Adam had what I call a constructive interpretation as he considered his situation. The way he looked at the challenge empowered him to be resilient, even coming out of it ahead. You could say he failed forward. He saw opportunity in the challenge and seized it. Even when the opportunity didn't unfold in the timeline he hoped for, he continued to pursue it until it became reality.

Vivian, on the other hand, had a destructive interpretation. She blamed herself for getting laid off, even though it was due to the financial peril in which her employer found itself rather than poor performance on her part. It was a business decision, not a personal one. Her interpretation caused her to lose confidence and motivation, which led to procrastination. Her lack of action put her in a poor financial position, leading to a hasty decision to take a job she didn't really want. Because she went into the new job doubting herself, she quickly began overworking in an effort to prove herself.

Constructive interpretations tell you the story about what happened, why it happened, and how you can use it to empower yourself. They enable you to see the opportunity in the challenge and be resilient through it. To create a constructive interpretation, you need to use an optimistic thinking style, which is a known predictor of success and resilience. Psychologist Dr. Martin Seligman calls this way of processing an optimistic explanatory style.[2] When good events happen, those with an optimistic thinking style explain the reasons for the event as personal, pervasive, and permanent. In other words, they believe (1) good things happen because they did something to make it happen, (2) good things can happen in other areas of their lives, and (3) good things can last forever. When bad events happen, those with an optimistic thinking style explain it in opposite terms. They see bad or negative events as external, specific, and temporary. They believe (1) it happened because of external forces more than personal ones, (2) the problem is specific and isolated, not pervasive, and (3) the problem is temporary.

When you choose a constructive interpretation, you not only believe that the situation will get better, but you choose solutions that move you forward in positive ways. With an optimistic thinking style, you believe you helped cause good events and therefore you can impact positive outcomes. You don't believe bad events are all due to character flaws, but rather to external factors, which you may be able to change or work around. For example, if a project went poorly, you may recognize that the timeline was too aggressive, that the resources were too limited to accomplish the task, or that the team lacked a key skill set. Rather than blaming, you recognize that these issues can possibly be addressed on future projects. You are not making excuses about why the project went poorly; you are looking for the opportunity to grow so that future projects are successful. You learn from the challenge and discuss how to adjust the goal or obtain the elements necessary to accomplish it.

On the other hand, someone with a pessimistic thinking style believes that when good things occur (1) they were due more to external forces than personal ones, (2) good fortune is specific and isolated, not pervasive, and (3) it's only temporary and difficult to replicate. But when bad events occur, those with a pessimistic explanatory style believe (1) they must have done something wrong or had a flawed innate trait for it to happen, (2) the problem will impact other areas of their lives, and (3) it will last forever.

When you notice a pessimistic thinking style underlying a destructive interpretation, your approaches to try solving the challenge may become counterproductive. Resilience is often elusive when hesitation, doubt, and procrastination hijack your decision-making. Rather than looking for the opportunity in the challenge, you may feel

REFRAME YOUR OUTLOOK

If you notice that you are struggling to overcome a destructive interpretation of an event or obstacle, use the following questions to coach yourself to adopt a constructive mindset instead:

- What is the opportunity in this challenge?
- What is the message for me in this?
- What will I have to do to come out of this better and not bitter?
- If the opportunity I want doesn't exist, what are my options for creating or pursuing an alternative path to my goal?

doomed by it. You can make a choice, however, when you notice that you're holding a destructive interpretation. You can choose to adopt a constructive one instead.

Let's look at several strategies you can take to develop positive yet realistic constructive interpretations that may help you reach your goal.

CREATE YOUR OWN OPPORTUNITY

When you keep hitting roadblocks as you travel toward your goal, sometimes being resilient means finding a different pathway. Failure offers many messages, one of which is "What might be an alternative path to your goal?"

I was reminded of this while watching a clip from an old BBC interview with Sylvester Stallone. Prior to starring in the blockbuster movie *Rocky*, Stallone had not landed major acting roles. In 1970, he had an uncredited appearance in the movie *M*A*S*H* and appeared as an extra in the movie *The Sidelong Glances of a Pigeon Kicker*. In 1971, he had a few more extra roles as a subway thug in Woody Allen's *Bananas* and dancing in a nightclub in *Klute*. By 1975, he had supporting roles in just a couple of other movies.[3]

On March 24, 1975, Stallone watched the Muhammad Ali vs. Chuck Wepner heavyweight championship fight held in Cleveland. It is one of only four fights in Ali's career in which he was officially knocked down in the ring, and yet Ali was still victorious in the long fight. After fifteen rounds, Ali knocked out Wepner and was recognized as the undisputed heavyweight champion. Three days later Stallone had finished the first draft of *Rocky*.[4]

Just let that sink in. Three days of focus produced the first draft of the screenplay of one of the most celebrated films in history. Of course, the real magic happens in the rewrite, he admits. But first, you must have something on the page to rewrite! And now he did. But his big goal was to play the lead role of struggling boxer Rocky Balboa, and he began pitching his script with that intention.

So after writing the role of Rocky Balboa to give himself the opportunity to play a leading role, Stallone refused to consider ceding the part to anyone else. "It was fairly presumptuous of you, wasn't it, to expect to be able to star in it because your career up to then had been small parts, right?" the BBC interviewer asked.

"It's kind of you to even say small," Stallone joked in response. "Yeah . . . I was mostly what is known as atmosphere. I was in the background or the guy, the drunk that was being stepped over in the gutter and other lame roles. But I felt that if I was going to go down, at least into professional obscurity, I wanted to at least have the opportunity to say to myself, *Well, you tried. You put your best foot forward and you didn't make it.* So that's what I guess you might say provoked me into writing the script because it wasn't something that I'd given a lot of thought to. I just knew that I had to do it one time."[5]

What Stallone decided to do was not presumptuous, in my view, but audacious and bold. The challenge he faced was achieving his acting dream, perhaps one of the hardest professions in the world in which to earn a living. Studies show that just 2 percent of actors make a living from acting.[6] A tiny fraction of those who make a living actually become well-known stars. When Stallone decided to write the script, he had been getting small roles for several years, but was not yet making a living from acting. He was struggling to pay his rent and buy food, and his wife was pregnant. At one point, he even sold his dog for forty dollars to help make ends meet. (He later bought it back for a whopping $15,000 when he hit it big.)[7] He knew that the odds of getting a shot at his goal would be much better if he created his own opportunity than if he waited for someone else to give him an opportunity. The goal was to write a movie in which he could play the lead role. That was the opportunity in his challenge.

Stallone was offered $265,000 for rights to the screenplay—the equivalent of $1.46 million today. However, the producers had other ideas for the lead, including Burt Reynolds, Ryan O'Neal, or James Caan as Rocky. At the time he was offered the deal, he says he had just about $106 to his name. That's about $625 in today's dollars.[8]

Just imagine. You've got $625 to your name and you're offered nearly $1.5 million for something you wrote. The only catch is, you'll have to give up on your goal of starring in it and agree to let some big movie star play the lead role. What would you do?

Stallone had a vision, and the producers' request was an obstacle to reaching it. He didn't lose sight of his desire to be the lead actor, even though it was tempting. In an astonishing move given his financial circumstances, Stallone refused to sell if he was not cast as the lead. The producers finally relented, but not before cutting the offer significantly, perhaps by as much as 90 percent. Multiple sources say he was paid $35,000 upfront for writing and starring in the movie, and made royalties on the profits after the movie was produced.[9] *Rocky* went into production in January 1976 with a budget of less than one million dollars. The movie premiered that December, catapulting Stallone to worldwide fame. *Rocky* became the highest-grossing movie of 1976, earning over $225 million worldwide.[10] The movie went on to earn ten Academy Award nominations, "including Best Actor and Best Original Screenplay, and won three Oscars: Best Director, Best Picture, and Best Film Editing."[11]

It's easy to dismiss such a monumental success as the brilliance or talent of someone we now know as a legendary star, but prior to *Rocky* scores of producers, agents, and directors had crossed paths with Stallone when he played bit parts in major television and movie productions. None of those decision-makers, including the studio executives who ultimately bought the rights to his screenplay, saw his potential the way Stallone did. If you went by his track record prior to *Rocky*, you might have assumed he should give up acting and pursue a different career. Instead, Stallone looked for the message and the opportunity in the challenge. He did so for the satisfaction of knowing that if he failed at his goal, at least he could say that he'd turned over every stone of possibility before giving up and moving on.

Stallone was strategic and realistic in writing a movie that played to his strengths. Remember, authenticity is a hallmark of resilience. In talking about the kind of role he decided to write in which he would be convincing as the lead, Stallone said, "I surely couldn't pass myself off as a lawyer in a three-piece suit. I just don't think I have that kind of appeal or whatever. So I wanted to make him much more basic, a man from the street. What kind of a man? An underdog. Being a professional fighter, I think, has that connotation to it."[12]

Stallone wasn't getting the opportunities he wanted so he created the opportunity. Resilient people think differently. They ask, *What options haven't I considered?* They find a way to work around or through the roadblock. To accomplish that often requires doing what others don't and using whatever resources they can access. Remember how we defined resilience in the first chapter? Resilience is a *system* you create that enables you to withstand and recover from difficulties and stressors. That system is an organized, three-part framework of

- adaptive skills (mainly, how you *think*)
- protective resources (relationships, education, experience, skills)
- preventive measures (precautions, good decisions)

The stronger your system of resilience, the more likely you are to accomplish a vision or overcome hardship and challenges.

Viewed from the resilience framework, we can see how Stallone used his adaptive skills, thinking in ways that moved him forward rather than keeping himself stuck. He approached his goal with an optimistic thinking style that did not interpret an absence of big wins as a sign that he was not capable of achieving a big vision. Instead, he looked for a different pathway to the goal. He used protective resources by tapping into relationships and writing skills that he'd developed. Before pursing acting in New York, Stallone had studied drama at the University of Miami and often spent time writing one-man shows and rewriting scenes from movies to practice his skills. Once he'd written a screenplay that actually interested Hollywood producers, he negotiated a deal that aligned with his vision, even though it meant a lot less money on the front end.[13] In making the excellent decision to hold on to his vision of starring in the film rather than accepting more money to release the role to another star, he exercised a preventive measure that paid off in the long run. By keeping his eye on the vision, he was not distracted by dollar signs that could have left the vision unfulfilled.

TAKE RESPONSIBILITY

There is an adaptive skill all resilient people have in common in the face of challenges and opportunities: They take responsibility. They own their choices. They acknowledge their mistakes. And by doing so they learn needed lessons and feel empowered to fix problems.

When I found myself at a low point in my life, going through a divorce at thirty-six, I teetered at times between feeling like a victim of circumstance and taking responsibility for what I wanted to do with my life as I moved forward. I was scared. I was angry. I was deeply sad. I was disappointed, and at first I was afraid to take responsibility by owning the vision I wanted most for my life. Since I had been a teenager, I had always pictured myself as an entrepreneur, wife, and mom. Growing up, I imagined myself a real-life Clair Huxtable from *The Cosby Show* sitcom—with a successful career, fun marriage, and five kids. But here I was, in my mid-thirties with a successful career, divorced with no children. It's not the way I planned it.

In my book *Where Will You Go from Here?*, I share about the moment the realization really hit that my marriage was over and my life was about to change drastically.[14] I was at home alone in my kitchen when suddenly I was overcome with sadness and panic as reality set in. I began crying, and the weight of devastation made my legs physically buckle. I leaned onto the counter as the tears flowed uncontrollably. What started as soft cries became loud wails from the depths of my soul. I had never felt so out of control of my emotions, and it startled me. Instinctively, I felt the urge to reach out to someone. Surely this was a breakdown of some sort, and I needed someone to witness it, console me, and maybe throw me a pity party. I didn't consciously think about what I wanted from another human being in that moment, but reflecting back, I think that was my motivation. I picked up the phone and called my mom, but I wasn't able to get the words out, just sobs and gibberish. At first, she thought I was in some sort of emergency situation like an accident. "Valorie! What's wrong? What happened?"

I responded with a flurry of pitiful predictions. "I don't know what I'm going to do. I feel like I'm going crazy! I can't believe this is happening! My life is over!" She knew I was going through a divorce, and having been through two of her own, plus brain surgery, major physical disabilities, and a host of other life-altering events, she was clearly not the right person to call for a pity party.

"You are not going crazy, and your life is not over!" she said emphatically, so as to jolt me out of my downward spiral. "Life and death are in the power of the tongue!" she said firmly but lovingly, quoting the biblical proverb about the power of your words.[15] She had my attention. I stopped rattling off all the doom-filled declarations.

"Now listen, you sound like you look pretty ugly right now," she continued with a hint of sarcasm that evoked the first chuckle I'd had in a long time. "Go wash your face, take a walk. It's a nice day outside. Call me when you come back."

It wasn't the tone or the pity party I'd called for, but it was exactly what I needed. I did what she said. I went to the bathroom and looked in the mirror. She was right. I looked pretty ugly, my eyes red and swollen, nose running, and mascara smeared. I splashed my face with water and blotted it dry with a hand towel. As her words echoed in my mind, they called forth my faith and strength. I did what she said and took a walk. I quieted my mind, breathing slowly and praying for courage and calm as I walked toward nearby Spa Creek to sit by the water for a few minutes. Ever since my early childhood when the Gulf of Mexico was my backyard on the Air Force base in Florida, water has always calmed me. I watched the small ripples and light bouncing off the water and pondered my mother's words. *I can't keep saying these awful things to myself,* I thought. *Where will it get me? I mean, I might feel like my life is over, but it's not. In fact, I'm getting a chance to start over—no guarantees of how it will go from here, but it's not over.*

As I headed back down the street to my house, I began to feel a shift in my spirit. It was a flicker of resolve, a decision emerging in my conscience about how I wanted to show up in this situation. When I went inside and called my mother back, I was able to talk from a stronger place. It wasn't that I didn't cry again—there were many more tears in the days and months ahead—but they didn't come from that "woe is me" place.

While it felt like the most devastating event of my life to that point, part of me felt relieved and hopeful. Two thoughts came to me that I'd not had before. The first was, *I will walk through this fire, but it will not consume me.* I knew I had a turbulent road ahead. I knew it would get ugly and unpleasant, but I told myself, *It is what it is.* In that moment, I took responsibility. *You've made a decision; now carry it through. You'll feel afraid. You'll second-guess. And you'll be all right.* I didn't focus on how unfair it felt or how life should have turned out differently.

I then coached myself with a question: *How do you want to show up in this situation?* It was a powerful question I had not considered while feeling sorry for myself. I had spent so much time ruminating on the previous six years that I couldn't get back—prime years of fertility that were gone. Now I faced the very real possibility that I might never bear children. I felt wronged and angry with myself for ending up in this situation. Have you ever been there? It's easy to be sucked into negative, deflating self-talk. It's hard to hope for the true desires of your heart because you fear disappointment.

But when I pondered how I wanted to show up, it felt like God whispered a reminder to me of my biggest strength—my faith. The end of my marriage was not just one of the biggest challenges I would face. It was actually an opportunity to walk out my faith.

Between all the negative emotions I was feeling, coupled with my fears of an uncertain future potentially devoid of the family life I'd always envisioned, what I wanted most was to not end up angry, wounded, and bitter. I didn't want what was happening to me to define me in a negative way. On the other side of the divorce, I wanted somehow to be better, wiser, and stronger. It was an optimistic and intriguing thought. And I admit it was also driven by the fact that I didn't want to lose any more of my life than I already had. This decision empowered me to take responsibility, learn the lessons being offered, find the courage to start my life over, and come out on the other side stronger and better than before.

How did I want to show up in this situation? My answer became a declaration and the second key thought I had not had before: *I will be better, not bitter.* In the years that followed, I kept that declaration in front of me as I did exactly that.

Self-pity is self-sabotage.

Taking responsibility began with five commitments I made to myself, which created a resilient shift in my thinking. They enabled me to make choices that aligned with the three pillars of adaptive skills, protective resources, and preventive measures. As you reflect on the challenges in which you seek to be resilient, consider how these commitments could strengthen and shift your thinking:

1. **I will not feel sorry for myself.** Self-pity is self-sabotage. It leads you to focus on the forces beyond your control, which leaves you feeling powerless to notice and take action toward the things within your control. As a result, when you feel sorry for yourself, you often remain stuck.

2. **I will not stare at the closed door.** It is tempting to look back at what was and imagine either how much better things used to be or what you might have done differently. But if you're looking backward, you can't see where you need to go from here. You cannot focus on creating a compelling vision that has the power to pull you forward.

3. **I will dig deep to find the courage I need.** In order to survive and thrive through challenges and change, you need to bravely move out of your comfort zone. You will feel fear, uncertainty,

and doubt. Courage empowers you to conquer a spirit of fear and move forward despite discomfort.

4. **I will direct my thoughts. My thoughts will not direct me.** We don't control the thoughts that show up, but we can control which ones we embrace and focus on. The most important asset you control is your thoughts. Pay attention to what you are thinking, and intentionally replace counterproductive thoughts with those that reflect your vision.

5. **I choose to believe all things can work together for good.** In the midst of challenges, it can be easy to decide all is doomed because of the unwanted situation you are in. But it is possible for good fortune and good opportunities to emerge from otherwise dreadful events and circumstances. Those blessings become obvious in hindsight, but it is powerful to believe good things will come in the midst of the challenge. Trust that it is possible to come out on the other side of your challenge better and not bitter.

With these commitments as my guide, I took responsibility to navigate my situation carefully and intentionally. I practiced controlling the controllable by choosing my thoughts intentionally. I tapped into the protective resources I was truly grateful to have, such as family and friends who supported me with wisdom and a soft place to land as I figured out my next steps. I left Maryland and moved south to the area of the country where most of the people I love and who love me have always been. I stayed with family in South Carolina for a summer while I figured out my next steps. Then I moved to Atlanta, where I also have quite a bit of family.

Once there, I began therapy, where I learned more about myself—particularly the codependent tendencies that had derailed my personal life. I set out to become mentally healthy and strong. I started running, something I really disliked but that I knew from my studies in positive psychology would release feel-good chemicals to help ward off depression. Running gave me time to process and think in solitude, and became a place where I gained clarity and vision. Each time I took a step in my running shoes, I also thought of it as a metaphor for moving forward. It made me stronger. With the five commitments as my guiding thoughts, a support system of family and friends, and regular exercise, I was able to proactively maintain much stronger mental health than I had when faced with significant challenges as a teen and twentysomething.

When you're living at the highest level of resilience and are thriving, you'll discover that challenges can provide an opportunity to grow as you recover, so that you can emerge from the difficulty better or stronger in some way than you were before. In this way, stressors are a matter of perception. If you reframe challenging circumstances, choosing a constructive interpretation that empowers you with hope and inspires action and resilience, your focus and energy can make the difficulty less overwhelming. Finding the opportunity in challenge cultivates hope, which produces positive emotion, motivation, and action.

To be clear, this is not about denying reality or ignoring your frustration or disappointment just so you can focus on the opportunity. This is embracing reality, allowing yourself to feel what you feel, but also intentionally choosing thoughts, creative approaches, and actions to help you make the most of the situation. It is choosing to believe that things can indeed work together for good, even if they emerge from a situation that isn't.

FAIL FORWARD

Failing Forward is an excellent book by John Maxwell with a title we can all aspire to.[16] You can guess the book's main idea. When you fail, rather than allowing it to be a setback, find a way to allow the failure to move you forward. See it as an opportunity to learn and grow. The problem with failing is that, too often, we don't see it as a "what" but as a "who." When failing is a "what," it's an event, something that happened: "I failed." When failure is an event in time, something different can happen in the future: "Next time, I can win." But if we view failure as a "who," we allow it to define us: "I am a failure." It becomes something to be ashamed of because we believe failure is who we are. Once we adopt that belief, we will fail again the next time because we see failure as a part of our character. When we feel ashamed of failing, we will attempt to hide our failures. We may deny they even happened or go to great lengths to make excuses for what happened: "It wasn't really a failure; look at all of the reasons why I couldn't win." We cast blame rather than taking responsibility and looking squarely at what went wrong so we can do something different next time. As a result, we miss the prime opportunity in every failure, which is to learn and grow from it. When we internalize failure, we pretend and defend, avoiding the kind of honest evaluation that can make us stronger, wiser, and better for the future.

So what can you do to find the opportunity in the challenge that failure offers? Harvard Law School professors Douglas Stone and Sheila Heen have a helpful take on the kind of attitude that can enable us to be resilient in the face of failure. "After every low score you receive, after each failure and faltering step" they advise, "give yourself a 'second score' based on how you handle the first score. . . . Even when you get an F for the situation itself, you can still earn an A+ for how you deal with it."[17]

To fail forward, what steps do you need to take?

- Acknowledge the failure.
- Determine what caused it.
- Ask yourself the following questions:
    - *What specifically did I fail at?*
    - *What is the most important lesson I learned from it?*
    - *Despite not reaching the goal, is there anything I did well? If so, what?*
    - *What can I do differently in the future to succeed at this?*

EMBRACE POST-TRAUMATIC GROWTH

Failing forward can be considered a form of post-traumatic growth, or PTG. Unlike post-traumatic stress disorder (PTSD), PTG is "positive psychological changes experienced as a result of the struggle with trauma or highly challenging situations. . . . PTG may feature positive changes in self-perception, interpersonal relationships and philosophy of life, leading to increased self-awareness and self-confidence, a more open attitude towards others, a greater appreciation of life and the discovering of new possibilities."[18] Of course, no one would choose to go through traumatic or highly challenging situations, but when you find yourself in them, knowing that positive growth is a potential outcome can actually lower your stress level and make you mentally stronger. It plants a seed, letting you know that you can grow through the challenge instead of just surviving it.

QUESTIONS TO PLANT SEEDS FOR NEW GROWTH

- Is there a highly challenging situation you are facing right now?
- What positive growth is possible through this season?
- What do you hope for?
- How do you want to show up?
- What do you want to learn?
- Looking back years from now, what will you wish you had done?

Even in the most difficult of challenges, there is an opportunity. I have seen this play out in my life. Going through a divorce made me more compassionate. I developed greater empathy for the pain of others. My faith was strengthened deeply, and navigating this situation helped me face my fear of disapproval and rejection. What unique opportunity does your current challenge offer? Just asking yourself this question empowers you to take ownership of the challenge and discover the opportunity in it.

CONSIDER NEW OPTIONS

When the most resilient people find that they keep running into seemingly insurmountable obstacles on the path to their goal, they ponder this question: *If I can't get there the traditional way, what other options could I consider?* Your answer may look nontraditional. Are you willing to entertain a nontraditional path? Creativity is an adaptive skill that is often born of necessity.

When sixteen-year-old gymnast Kaylia Nemour, who was born and trained in France, found herself in a dispute about training sites with the French gymnastics federation that would keep her from competing for France in the 2024 Olympics, Neymour decided to pursue an alternate path to the games. While her mother is French, her father's parents were born in Algeria. As a result, Kaylia was eligible for dual citizenship, which would qualify her to compete for Algeria. She competed in the Paris Olympics on the Algerian team and won a gold medal, becoming the first Algerian and African ever to win gold in gymnastics.[19] Her country of residence, France, won no medals in gymnastics at the competition.

Sometimes the opportunity in the challenge requires you to be flexible as you consider your options. Bend so you don't break. Be willing to open your mind to new options. Recognize that the path to victory simply may not look the way you imagined. Adaptability can be the skill that makes the difference between resilience or lack thereof. When I wrote my first book years ago, I wanted a major publisher to pick it up but decided to publish it myself because I knew the odds of getting published were 100 percent if I took that route, and about one percent if I waited for a major publisher to see my potential.

Perhaps the area in which you need to be more flexible is your relationships. For example, my vision for marriage and family didn't include marrying someone who already had kids. It wasn't a rigid rule; it just wasn't something I'd considered. I imagined meeting someone like me who didn't have children yet, but of course, by my late thirties, that was less likely than it had been in my twenties. When I met Jeff, I felt such peace about our relationship. I knew it was right, even though I'd never pondered the possibility of being a bonus mom. Adaptability meant opening my mind and heart to make space for this new and meaningful role in my life, as the girls were just five and eight years old when I came into their lives. Given my own negative experiences as a stepchild, I had strong feelings about what it meant to become a stepparent, and I was determined that the impact of me entering their already-existent family would be a positive one. Discovering my unique role as one of their four co-parents was an important part of my journey. It all started by opening myself to a path to marriage and parenthood that was outside of the vision I originally held.

What about you? When you think of the challenge you face right now that requires your resilience, how might you open your mind to alternative paths to your goal? How might creativity and flexibility empower you to "bend so you don't break"?

Coach Yourself

- What is the challenge you need to navigate right now?
- What would it look like to *survive* this challenge? What would it look like to *thrive*?
- What is the opportunity in this challenge?
- If you embraced that opportunity, what could it look like to thrive in spite of or as a result of this challenge?
- What are one to three actions that would help you seize the opportunity in your challenge?
- Which of the five commitments might be most important for you to make right now?
    - I will not feel sorry for myself.
    - I will not stare at the closed door.
    - I will dig deep to find the courage I need.

- I will direct my thoughts. My thoughts will not direct me.
- I choose to believe all things can work together for good.

Try This

- ☐ Look for the opportunity in your challenge. It could be the chance to try something new, reset, learn a lesson, stretch out of your comfort zone, slow down, or shift into high gear.
- ☐ Embrace the opportunity in your challenge. Of the one to three actions you chose when coaching yourself with the questions above, choose one that you will move forward with and set a date to begin.
- ☐ Share your plan of action with someone who will be supportive of your efforts.

SAY IT WITH ME:

"I look for the opportunity in my challenge."

RESILIENCE RULE #9

KNOW WHEN TO GRIT, KNOW WHEN TO QUIT

When I say yes to things I should say no to,
I have to say no to things I should say yes to.

KEY MESSAGES

- Resilience is more than just perseverance; it's the wisdom to know when to quit.
- Grit also requires grace.
- Purpose fuels perseverance, so get clear about yours.

"Never give up."

"Winners never quit, and quitters never win."

"Winning isn't everything; it's the only thing."

These are the quotes many of us heard while growing up. We learned that quitting is a terrible idea—something to always avoid. If you quit, it is something to be ashamed of. As a general rule, "never say never" is good advice. When it comes to resilience, though, it is sometimes bad counsel. There are exceptions to most rules, and it's wise to know when you need to make one.

What about the times you realize you started something you never should have? Or that the goal you set is superficial or not worth the cost in relationships, energy, or resources? Are you ever allowed to change your mind? When you gain newfound wisdom, are you allowed to set new priorities that align with your values? If you change course, are you just a quitter? And if so, does that mean you didn't "win"? Resilience requires perseverance, but your beliefs about perseverance, or grit, can actually sabotage your ability to be resilient.

During graduate school at the University of Pennsylvania, I had the opportunity to learn from celebrated experts in positive psychology. My professors were some of the most acclaimed researchers in resilience, positive emotion, strengths, happiness, and yes, *grit.* My graduate program was inspiring and thought-provoking, and one of the most fun educational experiences of my life. It also brought a bit of redemption for me. While I was disappointed to learn that the research on grit suggested I was part of a particular group that lacks resilience, I have come to understand that one ingredient can drive perseverance more than any other: purpose. Let me give you a little backstory.

An Auspicious Appointment

In the spring of my senior year of high school, I received a tremendous honor that arrived in a white catalog envelope with the name of a prestigious university and the words "Presidential Appointment" printed in navy blue letters on it.

No way! I thought. *This can't be.* By this point, I was pretty certain I had not gotten into this school. The lengthy application process had included a physical fitness test and interviews with military officers. I'd also had to submit proof of my leadership credentials, grade transcripts, and more. This college also required a nomination and appointment from a US senator, representative, the vice president, or the president. The good news for me was that presidential appointments were reserved for military brats—the children of veterans—and by this point, my dad had been on active duty in the Air Force for eighteen years.

When I opened the mystery envelope after school that afternoon, I pulled out a letter of acceptance to the United States Air Force Academy. My dad was stationed in South Korea that year, so I called him. It wasn't yet 6 a.m. in his barracks, but the men were up. The airman who answered the hallway phone was kind enough to go find my dad for me.

"Hi, Dad," I said when he picked up. "I'm sorry to call so early, but I have something to read to you that I think you're going to want to hear." As I read my dad the letter, he stayed quiet. "Did you hear me, Dad?" I said, wondering if we'd gotten disconnected.

When he responded, I realized he was quiet because he was so choked up by the news. I'd never heard my dad cry before. He was overwhelmed with emotion as he told me how proud he was. Then I heard him yell down the barracks, "My daughter got into the Air Force Academy!" I could hear his fellow noncommissioned officers yelling and clapping.

I smiled, grateful to hear his pride and excitement. Deep down, however, I felt a bit of hesitation. Being accepted was such an honor. But I was no longer sure the Academy was the right path for me. My parents were confident, though. And between their impending divorce and the financial hardships the separation had caused my family, the savings for my college education had been drained. I received offers of full or partial tuition scholarships from three other schools, but this was a full ride and a tremendous opportunity. My mom insisted I go. So I did.

To say it was a rough year is an understatement. My parents divorced during my first semester, I had surgery and three hospital stays, and I felt completely out of my element. I also spent most of the year on academic probation. By the end of my first year, I had decided to leave.

My college career had begun with a pretty dramatic—and somewhat traumatic—failure. I had stressful dreams about my first year of college for at least two years after it was over. If you had told me everything I was about to go through before I arrived on campus, I probably would never have attended. But I suppose that's often true of our difficult experiences. I had never struggled so much academically, and by the time I left, I really felt dumb. I doubted my intelligence. I lost all of my academic confidence, and I spent the next couple of years trying to prove to myself that I was still smart.

Nonetheless, I did feel good that I'd made it through that intense first year because I didn't want to quit before completing it. In the midst of this setback, I combined the adaptive skill of positive thinking with that of setting a goal to finish college—quickly. Though I'd already been a year ahead when I finished high school at seventeen, I raced through the remaining years of college, trying to overcompensate for my perceived first-year failures. I attended community college in California, where my mother had moved. Then I transferred to Florida State University, which offered me the same scholarship they'd given me out of high school. I graduated from college in three years, and at twenty, I entered graduate school at nearby Florida A&M University, one of the nation's historically black colleges and universities. I absolutely loved it at FAMU, experiencing for the first time what it felt like not to be a minority but in the majority. It was a rich experience for me, but I raced through that experience too. By twenty-one, I had a master's degree in journalism. At a time when I had finally begun to enjoy my college journey, it was over.

My push to achieve continued. I became a marketing director for a CPA firm before founding my own public relations firm. By thirty-four, I had written five books. When I went back to school thirteen years later to study applied positive psychology, I had the opportunity to learn from the illustrious researcher Dr. Angela Duckworth. She was one of my favorite professors and somehow made a class about research methods and statistics fun and engaging. A foremost researcher on grit, she's the author of a *New York Times* bestseller of the same name. *Grit* is a fascinating look at a particular type of perseverance unique to some of the most successful people in the world. She and her fellow researchers define *grit* as "passion and perseverance for long-term goals of personal significance."[1] One of her early research projects involved studying the behavior of cadets at West Point, the US Army's service academy, probing the differences between the cadets who punched out early and those who persevered to graduation.[2]

When I took the class, I was twice as old as the day I had become a cadet at the US Air Force Academy seventeen years earlier. But as I sat in class learning about her research, I was caught off guard by a topic that felt personal because of my own experience. My gut reaction was one of quiet shame. My thoughts went from excitement about learning to embarrassment about the past. *I guess I am one of the "ungritty" ones*, I thought.

As we discussed what separated the two groups of cadets, one student asked, "Was it related to their academic performance?"

Another pressed, "Did they find out what happened to these students after they left?"

As the discussion continued, I wanted to disappear under my desk. My classmates had no idea that that was my story, but it really rattled me. Until that moment, I'd believed that I *was* someone with grit. But this new narrative challenged the way I saw myself. Did I even belong in that room? Because the research sounded pretty definitive: The cadets who didn't make it lacked grit. They didn't stick with it. They weren't focused. They were not to be emulated.

After feeling defeated for some time, though, something within me pushed back. *This doesn't ring true for me,* I thought. *I didn't quit simply because I lacked grit. There had to be more to it than that.* For the past seventeen years, it had been clear to me that the Academy was simply not the place for me. I had no regrets about leaving. I hadn't been sitting around daydreaming about what my life coulda/woulda/shoulda been if I'd stayed. Not once. For the first two years after I left, I occasionally had nightmares that I was still there, but I was always relieved when I woke up and realized I was not. I never, however, daydreamed about being there. It wasn't meant to be, and it had to unfold the way it did. In fact, despite the stress from my parents' divorce and the medical issues I'd faced, the truth is that if I'd done well academically, I likely would have stayed.

Failure had actually pushed me in a new direction, one that freed me to discover who I was meant to be and what I was meant to do. It allowed me to embrace and leverage my natural talents and interests, such as writing and speaking. There is no question that the Air Force had been a great way of life for my family. For the first seventeen years of my life, it was all I knew. I was born on an Air Force base, my father retired from the Air Force, and my mother retired from the Army Air Force Exchange Service (AAFES), a multibillion-dollar retailer that serves US military bases worldwide. I'd never lived in a civilian household. Plus, the Academy was just a fifty-mile drive from our home in Colorado. It was a true honor to be there, but prestige and doing what my parents wanted wasn't enough to fuel perseverance. It wasn't my calling. And no matter how much I tried, I lacked the passion and purpose that some of my fellow cadets had. I still admire the grit and perseverance required, not only to graduate from a military academy, but to work in any capacity in the military. My respect and gratitude for those who serve are immense. What I know from my own personal experience, though, is that it was not *my* path. Understanding and honoring that fact opened the way for me to find my true calling.

Purpose Can Help You Course Correct

Purpose gives you a why that keeps you focused and persistent when things get tough. Purpose gives you the strength and fortitude to endure difficulties because you know exactly why you are doing something. You know it is tied to your unique assignment and the vision that propels you forward. It has personal significance to you. Without purpose, long-term perseverance doesn't just test you. It can break you. When making a decision about whether to persevere on a journey, first ask, "What purpose does perseverance fulfill here?" and "Why does that purpose matter to me?"

THE PURPOSE-PERSEVERANCE CONNECTION

- What purpose does perseverance fulfill here?
- Why does that purpose matter to me?

If your answers to these two questions fuel you to keep going, then persevere. If your answers leave you perplexed or drained, slow down. You may be at that fork in the road where a decision needs to be made about whether to stop or keep going.

Grit is more than sticking with a goal until you succeed. It is more than just perseverance. Grit is enabled by passion for a goal of personal significance. If you have no passion for something, and the goal doesn't hold significant personal meaning that is authentic to you and your interests, grit will be hard to achieve. In the face of significant challenges, grit is nearly impossible to maintain without significant emotional sacrifice.

Yet it can also take courage to make a change when you have been attempting to persevere in an area for which you have no passion. True resilience means deciding that you will align your decisions and choices with a sense of purpose. In fact, when you see that you are headed down the wrong path, it takes resilience to course correct. Your sense of purpose can give you the strength to make a change, risk disapproval, and overcome fears and uncertainty. Purpose will fuel your perseverance.

True resilience is deciding that you will align your decisions and choices with a sense of purpose.

Sometimes you must coach yourself to understand that your answers to two similar questions can be entirely different:

Is this a purposeful path?

Is this a purposeful path *for you*?

Hard versus Burdensome

Several years ago, as I was mulling over a decision that had been weighing heavily on me, I stumbled across these words in the book of Matthew during my quiet meditation. I'd read them before, but for some reason, the words took on new meaning that day:

> Come to me, all you who are weary and burdened, and I will give you rest. Take my yoke upon you and learn from me, for I am gentle and humble in heart, and you will find

> rest for your souls. For my yoke is easy and my burden is light.
>
> MATTHEW 11:28-30

I had been working on a project, and to be blunt, I dreaded the work. It wasn't that it was hard. Someone else might have loved it. But I didn't. It wasn't purposeful. It wasn't a good use of my strengths. It wouldn't lead to a better opportunity. It took up a lot of time that could have been better used elsewhere. This combination of facts made it more than just "hard" for me. It was a different feeling: This work felt burdensome. Burdensome wasn't just hard. It felt heavy and demanding—*too* heavy and demanding. It was completely draining because I'd run out of energy for it.

As I ran across those words from Matthew that day, it occurred to me that, although the things I am meant to do in my life may be difficult, they are not burdensome. God's yoke is easy and his burden is light, I was reminded. And with that insight, the decision about whether to continue this work became much easier. Someone else could do it better and more joyfully. I would trust that if something is meant for me to do, the burden will be light—even if the task itself is difficult.

Running a business, leading a team, or managing relationships may sometimes be hard and challenging, but they should energize you or at least feel meaningful and purposeful. This distinction between difficult and burdensome has guided me now for years. I invite you to take note of the key distinctions between activities that are hard and those that are burdensome:

1. **You're working hard and you're tired, but deep down, you're energized by the work.** When something is hard or challenging but you are energized by it, that can be a sign that you are right in the midst of your sweet spot. There is a certain gratification that comes from laboring at something aligned with your purpose. You can give everything you have and yet still have the energy to keep going.

2. **You feel stretched but not broken.** Difficult tasks and situations stretch you. They empower you to learn and grow and become more of the person you are meant to be. Growth, by its very definition, expands you into a bigger version of yourself.

3. **You are at peace even in the midst of the chaos.** Some seasons of life are very difficult, even chaotic. You look forward to getting through them, even when you feel uniquely equipped to handle them. Chaos can swirl around you, and yet you remain calm. You are at peace.

4. **There is purpose in the pain.** Difficult tasks and situations fulfill a purpose. Burdensome ones distract you from your purpose. Demanding but purposeful situations can transform you, give you clarity, strengthen relationships, and mature you so that you are better prepared for the future. They lead you toward your purpose. If you can see that by persevering, you'll find the reward to be worth it, stick with the challenging task. Making sacrifices for a greater purpose can make difficult tasks meaningful.[3]

How Strong Is Your Why?

When international track champion and four-time Olympian Chaunté Lowe combined her passion for track and field with her vision for getting to the Olympics, she relied on an underlying motivation that drove her discipline when the training was grueling. "I wanted to get out of poverty. I didn't want that to be my reality ever again," she remembers. "And as a teenager, when I looked all around me at the people who got out of poverty, the thing I saw they had in common was an education." Chaunté knew that excelling at track and winning state and national competitions in high school would get the attention of colleges who could give her scholarships and a ticket to the education that would get her to the goal.

Reaching her objective was sometimes painful. Because of how focused her coach was, training was demanding, and he expected consistency. Practices were grueling, often leaving her muscles burning, and she says she didn't always feel like going. Some of her teammates skipped practice when things got hard. They gave up. But Chaunté says, "I made a decision. It's going to hurt and I'm going to do it anyway." She knew she'd be spending her time doing something whether or not she went to practice. She might as well work toward something that would get her what she wanted from life—the chance to build a foundation of financial security that could unfold with the benefit of a good college education.

Chaunté intentionally used her adaptive skills, choosing thoughts that strengthened her—such as knowing she'd do the work even when it was painful. And she used those adaptive skills to work toward the protective resource of attaining a college education that would help her build the financial security she didn't have growing up. Purpose fueled her perseverance. And her perseverance paid off. Among the many opportunities she earned was a scholarship to Georgia Tech, one of the top universities in the nation. Chaunté graduated with a degree in economics the same year that she earned a bronze medal at the Olympics—her second of four consecutive Olympic appearances. Her why was the driver that earned her both the degree and the medal.

Zero In on Your Why

In your biggest battles, it is so important that you articulate your purpose. Zero in on your why. Purpose is like a compass that will point you in the right direction and then fuel your journey. On days when I felt like giving up on my vision as a writer, speaker, and entrepreneur, purpose always kept me going. For the first ten years of my journey in the work I do now, I often second-guessed myself. The work was often hard, and I wasn't making the money I'd hoped to make. I daydreamed about where I might be financially if I'd stuck with public relations and climbed the corporate ladder instead of pursuing the lonely, adventurous journey of business ownership. On occasion, I even perused job hunting sites and entertained the idea of abandoning ship on my dreams. But purpose always seemed to gently guide me back onto my path.

Eventually, I articulated that purpose so clearly that the second-guessing stopped. I realized that no amount of money would be worth abandoning what I believe I was put on the planet to do. Whatever I earned, I would learn to live on that, and I would have peace knowing that I was living life on my terms, doing exactly what I was called to do. I'd kept my living expenses relatively low for many years, and those choices essentially served as preventive measures that made it easier for me to keep persevering in my purpose long enough to finally begin to prosper.

Without a strong-enough why, you're more likely to give up in your hardest moments. Perseverance is challenging and takes discipline and a lot of energy. You'll be repeatedly tempted to give up, and when that happens, deep down you'll need an answer to this question: *Why should I keep going?*

The answer is found in your personal mission. In my book *Rich Minds, Rich Rewards*, I invite readers to create a personal mission statement. For instance, mine is: "To create and enjoy a fulfilling, prosperous, and generous life, and to inspire others to do the same." Keep your statement brief, action-oriented, and unique to *you*!

To craft your own mission statement,

1. Begin with active verbs describing what you want to do through your life: "My personal mission is to __________ and __________." (Mine are *create* and *enjoy*, but you may want to choose more than two words.)

2. Then name the purpose, philosophy, cause, principle, or value that's most important to you. (Mine is "a fulfilling, prosperous, and generous life.")

3. Finally, choose the group or cause you desire to affect in a positive way. (Mine is to have a positive impact by inspiring "others" to also live well.)

You now have the recipe for your mission statement!

Those who persevere do so for a reason. They know their purpose and why they must persevere. That purpose fuels their perseverance. To be resilient, you must know if there is a greater purpose in persevering through your challenge, and if so, what that purpose is. Persevering for its own sake is not always wise, but persevering for a purpose brings meaningful results.

One of my favorite positive psychology tools is the VIA Character Strengths Survey. Developed by the late Dr. Chris Peterson, my capstone advisor in graduate school, in collaboration with Dr. Martin Seligman, it is an assessment of strengths. VIA stands for "Values in Action," underscoring the fact that our strengths are innate values that we leverage whenever we engage in the world. The VIA classification of twenty-four character strengths, which is based on universally celebrated strengths across cultures in more than seventy-five countries, identifies spirituality, which is connected to faith and sense of purpose, as one of the unique character strengths.[4] Those who have this strength have strong beliefs about the higher purpose and meaning of life and knowing where they fit within the larger scheme of things.

Even if you do not naturally gravitate toward a sense of purpose, you can cultivate this strength by pinpointing your why. You can leverage that purpose to generate energy that motivates, inspires, and literally moves you forward. It just so happens, for me, that purpose is my top strength, which likely helps explain how compelled I have felt at critical points in my life to give up on things that didn't feel purposeful and persevere in things that do. Even if it is not among your top strengths, though, your purpose will always lie under the surface, nudging you and fueling you to persevere in the right direction. The absence of purpose will prod you as well, giving you the wisdom to know when it's time to let go. Remember these simple ways to listen for purpose in a situation:

- Sometimes you need to stick to it. You are almost there. There's a difference between "hard" and "burdensome."

- Sometimes you need to recognize that the season for something is over, and it is time to do things differently. That's not giving up. That's entering a new season. Persevering with the old in a new season will mean forgoing the new. You must change the narrative and make room by letting go.

- Sometimes you discover that you never should have embarked on a journey in the first place. In those instances, persevering is not the goal if there is no purpose in doing so. Forgive yourself. Look for the lesson. Don't just *go* through the experience; *grow* through it.

- A lack of purpose is a sign. Do not ignore it. It may be an indication that something is not worth pursuing or a signal that you need to tweak the vision or goal so that it is aligned with a sense of purpose.

A WORD FOR WOMEN

I want to say a word to women about gritting and quitting. Men, you're welcome to listen in.

Though I suspect you already know this, even if not at a conscious level, many women carry an invisible load. Naturally alert to the needs of others, women are shouldering their own loads, often along with those of others. It's typically the woman who's responsible for the safety and care of an aging parent. It's often the mom, whether she works outside the home or not, who's buying the groceries, scheduling the doctor's appointments, arranging rides to and from soccer practice, and planning family vacations. And because the world insists that you need to be handling all of this, I am giving you explicit permission—that perhaps you've never received—to *choose* between gritting and quitting. For you, being resilient means that you are owning that choice. And because I'm pretty sure you've likely already nailed *grit,* I'm asking you to give yourself permission to *quit* when it's the best thing for you.

When your children become capable of washing their own clothes? You get to quit. You get to assign that job to them.

When you're in a partnership that is death-dealing? You get to quit. You do not have to stay in a destructive, soul-crushing relationship.

When you've built your business and you want to step back to spend more time with your family? You get to quit. And quitting may simply mean that you continue to do the things that *only* you can do and hire someone to do everything else.

When you're overwhelmed by the needs of an aging parent? Make a plan because if you don't, gritting can deplete you to the point that you cannot give the care that's needed. Quitting, in this case, might mean accessing other resources—accepting help from family and neighbors and then tapping every resource available, whether through insurance, social services, or hired help a few hours a week if you can afford it—to get the job done.

You get the idea. Because the world has taught women to subvert their own needs, I'm inviting you to be very intentional about when it's right to grit and when it's right to quit.

"Never Give Up" Is Awful Advice

Being doggedly persistent about the wrong goal is not authentic resilience. It is not adaptability. It often stems from stubbornness, pride, and fear. Yes, there are times when giving up demonstrates an absence of grit. But giving up can also mean the presence of wisdom. The courage to step down, step away, or step aside can be a sign of profound resilience. What feels like defeat may actually be a triumph.

When I made the decision to give up on IVF, I wasn't giving up on my dream of motherhood. My husband and I chose another path, one that felt purposeful for us. For someone else, patient persistence and repeated rounds of treatment could be the purposeful means to their goal. In our quiet time of prayer, we did not feel called to continue. No matter how many friends or family encouraged us not to give up on IVF, I didn't want to do it again. So we didn't. Know yourself and your why. Let peace guide your decisions.

When I walked away from a full-time job as a marketing director to pursue my entrepreneurial dream to run a public relations firm, fear of failure definitely whispered doubts. *Are you sure you want to quit your job?* My answer was yes. Quitting would be necessary if I was going to head into the future as a business owner rather than an employee. Then when I walked away from a successful business in public relations to pursue the work I do now, it was following my purpose that called me forward.

Sometimes quitting is the most resilient thing you can do. Something doesn't have to be wrong in order to be the wrong thing . . . for you. Knowing when to walk away and then finding the courage to do so is powerful. Quitting the wrong thing is often the only way to make space for the right thing. As you grow and learn, you become wiser. Sometimes the wisest decision you can make is to stop doing something that serves no purpose for you and begin saying yes only to the people and things that serve a meaningful purpose. When you take this approach, persevering becomes so much easier. Purpose becomes leverage that lightens the load of perseverance. It provides fuel for the long journey and gives you the grace to do hard things.

Quitting the wrong thing is often the only way to make space for the right thing.

When my mother came home after two months in the hospital following life-saving brain surgery after a massive brain aneurysm rupture, she could barely speak, couldn't sit up on her own or walk, and faced a host of other problems. The prognosis was very discouraging, and she would need to find the will to live and recover. But she tells me she kept thinking about one thing during her hardest days. "I knew you would be okay," she told me. I was twenty-eight and self-sufficient. "But I had to make it for Wade," referring to my much-younger brother, who was eight at the time. In other words, Wade was the purpose that fueled her perseverance. He was a reason to fight for her life.

The resilience you need may, in fact, have life-or-death consequences. In most instances, though, the stakes aren't quite so high, yet the principle still applies. Your reason for persevering must hold meaning for you if you are to have the grit to stick with it through the most difficult of challenges. Perseverance for its own sake is not a strong-enough purpose for enduring difficulties. Purpose must come before perseverance.

When you've done something a long time, you can fall into the trap of believing things always need to stay the same. But sometimes it's time for a change. The evidence of that is often in the energy and purpose you sense for the path you are on. I call that energy and purpose "grace."

There's a coaching question I love to ask when someone is struggling to figure out whether they should stay on their current path or give themselves permission to change course. When it comes to decisions about what you commit your time to, ask yourself this: *Do I have the grace to do it?*

If the answer is yes—you do have the energy or purpose for it—keep going. Stay the course. It has purpose. And with grace, you'll muster the energy for it. Even when a path is hard, when you have the grace to do it, it's a sign. When the grace leaves, that's a sign too. So if your answer to the

TO DO OR NOT TO DO

When clients wonder whether they should continue to pursue a particular goal, I recommend they run through the following exercise:

- Identify the goal, opportunity, or challenge.
- Clarify your purpose in pursuing it.
- On a scale of 1 to 10, how aligned is the goal with your purpose?
- If you're satisfied with how aligned it is with your purpose, do it. If you're unable to give it a high rating, you may need to tweak it or choose one of these three options:
  - Delay it (if the timing, but not the purpose, is off).
  - Delegate it (if the task is purposeful—but you are not the best one to carry it out).
  - Delete it (if it does not serve a meaningful purpose or *no longer* serves a meaningful purpose).

question "Do I have the grace to do it?" is no, give yourself permission to make a shift.

If you are saying yes to things you should say no to, then you are saying no to things you should say yes to. Maybe it's time for a change—either by saying no or by taking on a new challenge that will grow you into the person you need to be in this season. If you pursue commitments and opportunities that aren't meant for you, you might just be blocking someone else from getting the opportunity and experience. Don't be afraid to reevaluate your commitments and make some changes. Grace can be your guide.

These steps will help ensure that you say yes only to the right things.

In small decisions and big ones, small goals and a monumental vision, resilience is strengthened by a sense of purpose. Let go of the idea that quitting is always bad. While sometimes quitting is not the resilient thing to do, at other times quitting is absolutely the wisest, most resilient choice you can make. Resilient people learn to discern the difference.

Coach Yourself

- In what area(s) are you finding the way forward hard or challenging right now?
- Is the challenge burdensome or is it just "hard"? Hard means you have the grace to do it even though it is difficult to achieve. Burdensome means you do not have the grace to do it, whether it's hard or not.
- What is the purpose of persevering in this challenge?
- On a scale of 1 to 10, how meaningful is that purpose to you in this season?
- What is the message to you in the rating you gave to the last question?
- How do you want to move forward in light of your answers to these questions?

- ▶ What next steps will you take?
- ▶ What resources or people could make those steps easier?

Try This

- ☐ Identify the purpose in persevering through your challenge.
- ☐ Once you identify the purpose, clarify whether the purpose is strong enough to fuel your perseverance or whether the goal or timing needs to be adjusted.
- ☐ If the purpose is strong enough, do it. If not, consider these three options:

  Delay it (if the purpose is strong, but the timing is off).

  Delegate it (if it is purposeful, but not purposeful for you to personally handle it).

  Delete it (if it does not serve a meaningful purpose or *no longer* serves a meaningful purpose).
- ☐ Put purpose before perseverance. Do not persevere for its own sake, but because there is a clear purpose in doing so.

SAY IT WITH ME:

"Purpose fuels perseverance."

RESILIENCE RULE #10

CLOSE YOUR ENERGY GAP

Discover the real reason you get burned out and learn how to replenish your energy the right way so the cycle stops repeating itself.

KEY MESSAGES

- Your energy level must match the level of your vision, or you'll burn out.
- Self-care and self-compassion are critical energy boosters.
- Negative is more powerful than positive, so carefully cultivate the positive.

I'll never forget the first time my dad let me drive his spare car to school. It was the first—and last!—time I ever ran out of gas. I'd had my license for about three weeks and kept bugging him to let me drive "Flo," the twelve-year-old fluorescent yellow Volkswagen Rabbit he'd bought to avoid wear and tear on his main car when driving on those frequent snowy Colorado days. Finally, he relented. My guess is that when he said yes, he imagined me driving to school, staying for cheer practice afterward, and then heading home. Although he didn't specifically ask for my itinerary, I'm pretty sure he didn't plan on me doing everything I did after school that day.

Excited about the freedom of having the car, I let all my friends know that I'd driven to school. Several asked for a ride home. It turned out that I didn't have practice that day, so I happily answered, "Sure! I can give you a lift!" But first, we hung out, stopping to get a bite to eat at Taco Bell. One friend lived in the neighborhood farthest from the school, in the opposite direction of the other two friends in the car. After I dropped off my three friends, I decided to go to the mall where I worked. Even though I was off that day, I found a reason to go.

By the time I headed home, it was getting late, probably close to 7 p.m. That's when I noticed a red light on the dashboard. The gas tank was on *E*! I had no idea how long the red light had been on. I'd probably had a third of a tank when my dad handed over the keys, but driving all over suburban Denver, I'd used almost all of it up. *No problem*, I thought. *I'll just stop and get some gas.* I pulled into a gas station for fuel, and that's when I realized I had an even bigger problem. The car required a second key to open the gas tank, and I didn't have it!

I was just a few miles from home, so I resumed driving, holding my breath and praying to make it. That's when I felt a sensation I have vowed never to feel again: the futile feeling of pressing on an accelerator and feeling no acceleration. I kept pushing with my foot, urging the car forward to no avail. I had no reserves; the car was completely out of gas. Something similar happens on your journey in life, especially during challenging times. And it brings us to this rule of resilience: "Close your energy gap."

When you have big goals and big challenges, it requires a lot of fuel to power through to your destination. If you don't pay attention, not only will you end up on *E*, but you may also use up any reserves you have and completely run out of gas. You must replenish your reserves and then refill your tank again and again so you don't burn out or give up.

Replenish and Refill

It is easy to underestimate just how much energy it will take to fuel your vision. And even if you have enough reserves to push through right now, your vision will eventually outdistance your stamina if you don't replenish your energy. One of the best ways to evaluate whether you need to boost your energy level is to rate both your energy and the vision or challenge in front of you. A challenge that is a 10 cannot be accomplished if your energy is at a 6. You might make some progress, but at some point along the journey, you'll stall. If you don't recognize that a lack of fuel for the journey is the reason you're at a standstill, you'll attribute your mistakes, lack of motivation, and slow progress to other factors. You may even beat yourself up: *I'm lazy. I'm unmotivated. I just can't get it together.* But what if it isn't any of that? What if it is simply that you are exhausted and need a break? What if you underestimated the sheer amount of effort and grit it would take to weather the challenge and get to the goal?

THE STRUGGLE IS REAL

Ashley couldn't figure out why she was starting to struggle to keep up with her workload. It had not changed much over the year, but she found herself getting behind on deadlines and taking longer to do her work. She'd sit down at her desk to tackle her assignments, but she struggled to organize her to-do list and stay on task. This had not previously been a problem.

During a coaching session, I asked her, "What changes have impacted you this year?"

At first, she couldn't think of anything. But when I asked her to consider her levels of energy—mental, emotional, and physical—she paused to reflect.

"You know this lack of energy isn't just showing up at work," she said. "It's happening with managing my household too. I'm just less organized and motivated than I used to be, especially in the last six months."

As Ashley considered the changes during that time frame, it occurred to her that it correlated with two things: surgery she'd had seven months earlier for a torn ACL and her young nephew coming to live with her while her sister was deployed overseas for a few months. While her nephew was doing well, she'd been forced to make big changes to her schedule. The many adjustments and coordination to organize her everyday life around his needs had required a lot of mental energy. She also drew on her emotional energy to support him through the change and homesickness.

The recovery from her surgery had created an unexpected drop in her physical energy. Ashley had been disciplined about her workouts, but when surgery temporarily disrupted that routine, she also lost the boost in energy that working out gave her. Prior to surgery, she had used her daily morning time on the elliptical machine to plan out her days, dictate and send emails, and keep up with friends and family. When the workouts stopped, so did this informal planning time, leaving her more hurried and less organized throughout the day. Around the time she recovered physically, her nephew came to stay, so she had never gotten back to her workout routine.

I had Ashley reflect on the required energy to feel successful in this new season and the available energy she had. Using the definition of required energy as (1) the amount and intensity of effort, (2) the period of time she needed to exert the effort, and (3) the circumstances and commitments that impact her capacity, she realized that her required energy was now about a 10. Just six months earlier, she estimated it had been about a 5 or 6. She'd been cruising along in her personal and professional life without many demands and with plenty of free time. Back then, she'd had only herself to take care of. When she considered her available energy in light of taking care of her nephew, recovering from surgery, and lacking time for the exercise that had given her such a physical, mental, and emotional boost, she realized that her available energy had dropped from about a 9 to a 4 or 5.

This reflective exercise was eye-opening. Ashley was finally able to acknowledge that she had experienced some significant changes—and that they were creating the challenges that plagued her. She'd been beating herself up, attributing her exhaustion and failure to stay on top of things to her lack of organization, but she now realized that the expectations she'd put on herself were unrealistic. "I've always been called a superwoman who can get a lot done. I'm not used to feeling so stressed and behind on everything," she explained. I invited Ashley to try self-compassion—talking to herself the way she'd talk to a best friend if they were going through the same challenges. "I wouldn't beat them up about it," she told me. "I'd point out how much they've got on their plate in the midst of recovery from surgery! And I'd probably tell them to take some time off to rest and get caught up."

Ashley knew what she needed to do. She decided to control the controllable, starting by reintroducing the exercise that had always given her physical energy, time to organize her thoughts, and a needed emotional boost. We brainstormed a plan so she could get back to her physical fitness routine, even though her schedule now needed to accommodate her nephew. She carved out some time early in the mornings, before he got up, and she went to bed about forty-five minutes earlier so she'd get the same amount of sleep. Within just a few weeks, she noticed the impact on her productivity at work and at home.

HOW FULL IS YOUR TANK?

Using the self-care framework I created, I asked Ashley to listen to what her life was telling her and then honor what she heard. Too often, we ignore the signals that are sending messages about our need to take better care of ourselves. You can use this same framework. Simply do two things:

1. **Listen.** What circumstances, situations, or changes in your life or work may be signs that you need better self-care? For example, you may be trying to balance new responsibilities at home or work, or you may be dealing with new challenges to your health, finances, or relationships. Frequent headaches, exhaustion or irritability, forgetfulness, chronic lateness and missed deadlines, and no time for leisure, social fun, or workout routines may be signals that your reserves are dangerously low.

2. **Honor.** It's not enough to listen and notice what is calling for your attention. You must also honor what you hear by doing something about it. What could you do to honor what you are sensing in these areas where you are depleted? Whether it's setting boundaries, looking for small pockets of free time in your daily routine, or brainstorming with a friend, neighbor,

or spouse about how you might work in some breathing room for each other, finding some simple ways to honor your need for rest and rejuvenation really is possible.

What's Your Energy Gap?

The need for resilience grows when you don't have the resources to meet the stressors you face. One of your most important resources is energy. It fuels your ability not only to keep going, but also to be consistent, creative, and committed.

The bigger your challenge, the bigger your commitment must be to doing what's needed to meet it. And the bigger the goal, the more energy it takes to achieve it. Whether you're using physical, mental, or emotional energy, it can be easy to underestimate just how much you need to get to the goal. When you are accurate in your assessments of what's really holding you back, you can more effectively determine the steps you need to take to create a breakthrough.

When you think about your current challenge and the outcome you want to experience, what level of energy will match the level of the challenge before you? If your challenge level is greater than your energy level, you have a gap to close in at least one of these areas: mental energy, emotional energy, and physical energy.

Let's look more closely at the three types of energy so you can identify where you have an opportunity to replenish yours.

MENTAL ENERGY

Mental energy is the energy required to perform cognitive tasks such as problem-solving, decision-making, focusing, and maintaining self-control. Just as you need physical energy to lift something heavy or run a distance, you need mental energy to carry the mental load of tasks that require thinking and processing information.

Your mental energy affects mood, cognition, and motivation. When it is depleted, you can become easily distracted, unable to focus, or even irritable and unmotivated. In my early studies in positive psychology, two concepts shed light on chronic problems that depleted my energy: decision fatigue and goal fatigue. Both are real! And every time I speak on these concepts to audiences around the world, there is collective head nodding, indicating just how much they resonate with what I describe.

Decision fatigue occurs when you become mentally exhausted by the sheer number of decisions you need to make. Goal fatigue is very similar. Studies show you have a finite amount of mental energy, and reaching for a goal or making a decision depletes some of that energy.[1] The more goals and decisions, the more depleted you become. If you do not replenish that energy, eventually you run out. When that happens, you may experience burnout, frustration, overwhelm, or apathy. Opportunities that used to excite you now drain you. And when new challenges appear, you feel unable to conquer them.

Whether you are managing people, running a business, or dealing with a complicated health challenge, be aware that making good decisions that empower you to be resilient through a challenge takes a lot of mental energy. When that energy is depleted and you are unable or unwilling to replenish it, you will find it harder to make good decisions. Your mood and attitude toward your challenge and the decisions that must be made may become more negative. You may become irritated by questions from others because you are being asked to make yet another decision. Even small requests may begin to cause stress and irritability.

Decision fatigue and goal fatigue are just two of the ways your mental energy gets taxed. One of the most insidious ways mental energy undermines your ability to be resilient is willpower. When you take on something challenging, discipline is one of the most important traits for success. Research has even shown that the ability to exercise self-control in childhood is a better predictor of future success than grades or standardized test scores.[2] It's not a surprise, considering that habits such as studying require discipline and the ability to tune out the distraction of more interesting pursuits in order to do what is necessary in the moment. But willpower is a finite resource that requires a great deal of mental energy.

When you repeatedly have to make difficult choices and trade-offs, the reality of finite mental energy becomes more pronounced. For example, if money is an issue and you are continually having to choose which purchase is a higher priority, the mental fatigue can be devastating. So exhausted by the need to be constantly disciplined in your spending, you may succumb to the temptation of one bad moment of overspending, sabotaging a month of good choices in the process. With no cushion to make up for that bad choice, you may dig a hole that requires even more discipline and difficult decisions, further wearing down your mental energy. This vicious cycle can make it difficult to bounce back and be resilient.

Goal fatigue occurs when you are either pursuing too many goals simultaneously or do not replenish your energy between goals and deadlines. When you reach a goal, it should be like getting to the destination on a road trip. You don't immediately start driving back home. Hopefully, you have a chance to stay and enjoy your destination for a while. And even if you do turn around and head back quickly, you refuel or charge up before getting back on the road. The same should be true when you meet deadlines and milestones. Savor the achievement by celebrating it. Rest a bit, if possible. And then when your energy is replenished, get going again. This approach is important with small achievements throughout your day as well as major milestones. Break your tasks into bite-size chunks and take breaks or reward yourself when they're completed. With major milestones, plan major breaks, rewards, or periods of rest and recovery when you achieve them. Remember, the bigger the challenge, the more energy you need to navigate it.

EMOTIONAL ENERGY

Emotional energy is the energy that is driven by your feelings, including your mood, motivation, passion, and enthusiasm—or lack thereof. While mental energy is required for cognitive tasks like focus and decision-making, emotional energy is spent by anything that impacts how you feel. They are interwoven, but different.

How you feel can strongly influence what you choose to do or not do. In fact, positive emotion can be a predictor of success. Research shows that when we feel good or happier, we are more likely to choose bigger goals, persevere toward those goals, and achieve them.[3] We may see more options and make better decisions.

In fact, just before I started to write this section on emotional energy, mine was thrown off. Go figure. When I took a break from writing for fifteen minutes, my plan was to sit and relax in the recliner near my desk while listening to a little smooth jazz. But I got antsy and decided to check email on my phone. Bad idea. My assistant had forwarded an email from our general email account, where someone had gone on our website and filled out the "contact us" form. This person claimed to be a police detective.

My assistant simply said, "I wanted to run this by you. This could be a phishing scam, but I thought it was worth passing along before ignoring or taking action."

I scrolled down in the thread to see an email from a police detective in another state asking for a mailing address for a subpoena. I immediately began to think of wild, irrational scenarios. Is someone taking legal action? If so, who? And what for? I was racking my brain for reasons we'd be getting a subpoena! This sent me down a rabbit hole of trying to confirm whether the message was legitimate. A quick search confirmed that the email address extension, in fact, matched the email address for public employees that work for that city. It was real, not a phishing scam. I texted our lawyer and my husband. I should have stopped at that point to get back to work and deal with the matter later. It wasn't urgent. But I couldn't focus because I was so curious about that email. My fifteen-minute break turned into an hour, culminating in a phone call from my husband who, unbeknownst to me as I was imagining a court battle to defend myself against untrue allegations, got to the bottom of it by looking up the number to the police department and calling the detective.

We were not being sued, nor were we in any sort of trouble. A stolen credit card had been used in an online transaction in our store.

It was an aggravation, but nothing that needed to involve me. But now, I'd lost more than an hour of time and lost my morning focus!

Have you ever been there? Most of the time, you don't lose emotional energy because of something as dramatic as an email from a police detective who wants to send you a subpoena, but because of an interruption from someone who calls or stops by your desk, the rude interaction that ruins your mood, or the temptation of email chimes or social media posts. Emotions that sour for any reason can keep you from maintaining your focus and staying consistent. Checking email while working on something that requires focus is often not a good idea. It drains mental energy, and depending on what lands in your inbox, it can shift your emotional energy in a negative direction. Your emotional energy can also be disturbed by relationship challenges, losses, disappointments, and betrayals.

Negative emotions, research shows, are much more powerful than positive emotions. On average, it takes three positive interactions to undo the effects of one negative interaction.[4] Your negative emotions make you less able to deal with challenges and adversity. Your scope of thinking narrows, making it harder to see options and make decisions.

Sensitivity to the negative is, in part, how we are wired to survive. We need to see threats and danger clearly so that we can protect ourselves. In fact, the prospect of a negative outcome on the horizon can motivate you to make changes to prevent that outcome from becoming reality. But there are limits to the motivation that can be sustained only by negative emotions, which can make you more hesitant, anxious, and pessimistic in the face of challenges. Because of this, negative emotional energy makes it harder for you to bounce back and persevere. In fact, too much negativity can cause you to develop what psychologists call a negativity bias. This means that your mind zeros in more quickly on the negative and is less likely to see the positive. For example, have you ever had a difficult time in a relationship and suddenly all you can see about the other person are the negative things they've done? When someone points out something positive, you reject it because it seems almost irrelevant when compared to their faults. That's negativity bias. In order for such a relationship to recover, a shift toward the positive is essential.

PHYSICAL ENERGY

Your physical energy is about how your body feels and how your health impacts the way you can show up in your life. Are you tired or energetic? Are you ill or well? Can you keep up with the physical demands of your challenges or are you worn out, slow, and weak? All of these factors impact your resilience, for better or worse.

The challenges you face mentally and emotionally can take a toll on your physical health. You might remember that, when I shared earlier about my mother's brain aneurysm, I mentioned we were discussing a stressful topic when the blood vessel in her brain burst.

She had a custody hearing scheduled for the next week as a part of her divorce, and it was all she could think and talk about. In fact, when I took a break in the ICU waiting room the next morning, two of her team members were sitting there anxiously. They said that when they arrived at work that morning and learned about my mother's aneurysm and subsequent brain surgery, several coworkers told them, "Lee was very anxious and distracted yesterday. We didn't know she'd been going through so much." My mom was just forty-nine, and the brain aneurysm changed her life dramatically. It's possible she would have had an aneurysm even if she had not been under such stress, but I doubt it. The pressure she felt, and the fact that we were talking on the phone when she felt the blood vessel burst, are likely not coincidences. Mental and emotional stress can wreak havoc on your physical health. Without that, it is difficult to consistently show up with the energy to adapt, rally your resources, or make wise preventive choices.

My hope is that you never encounter a devastating physical health issue, but all of us face exhaustion, sleep deprivation, and temporary illness at times. When that happens, take into account the impact on your energy. You may need to reset your expectations, ask for help, or make adjustments that reflect your current reality. If you don't, you may find it harder to sustain your normal pace and your "best" may not be what it normally is.

When you look at those three categories of energy, how are you doing in each area? Does your energy level match the level of the challenges before you? Have you noticed yourself stalling or spinning your wheels? Perhaps there is an energy gap that needs to be closed, giving you the boost you need to keep moving forward or even jump-start your efforts.

Energy Self-Assessment

To assess your energy gap, rate two factors: (1) the energy level you need to navigate the challenge and get to the goal (your "required energy") and (2) the energy level you currently have available (your "available energy"). Before you begin, keep in mind that it can be tempting to rate your energy based on what you *want* it to be rather than what it actually is. Remember Resilience Rule #7, "Don't pretend, don't defend," and resist that temptation. Honest answers will give you the information you need to take actions that will make you more resilient.

Before you begin, determine the challenge you want to tackle.

1. REQUIRED ENERGY

To estimate the energy it will take to successfully navigate the challenge you just identified, rate the following areas and then average them to determine a number on a scale of 1 to 10. Use the questions under each factor to help you estimate.

___ The amount and intensity of effort that will be required

___ The length of time you must exert that effort

___ The capacity you have to put forth that effort, given your other current commitments, circumstances, and resources

Based on the average of your answers above, what is your required energy level?

2. AVAILABLE ENERGY

To estimate the mental, emotional, and physical energy you currently have, rate the following three areas and then average them to determine a number on a scale of 1 to 10. Use the questions to help you think through and determine an accurate rating.

YOUR MENTAL ENERGY AND CAPACITY

___ How well are you able to focus and exercise the self-control needed to meet your goal?

___ How much mental energy do you have to think, strategize, and maintain consistency in your effort to navigate the challenge and reach your vision?

___ What other commitments, circumstances, or mental challenges are impacting your mental energy and capacity?

Based on how you answer the above questions, how would you rate your mental energy on a scale of 1 to 10?

YOUR EMOTIONAL STRENGTH AND STABILITY

___ Are you experiencing any emotional upheaval right now due to circumstances, events, or changes in your life or work?

___ Are your emotions stable or are they impacting your ability to push through fears and work consistently toward goals?

___ Do positive emotions outweigh negative ones in your life right now?

Based on how you answer the above questions, how would you rate your emotional energy on a scale of 1 to 10?

YOUR PHYSICAL ENERGY AND STRENGTH

___ What is your physical energy and capacity? Do you feel tired or energized? Weak or strong?

___ Are you currently injured, sick, or dealing with any health challenges, or are you strong and fully capable from a health perspective?

Based on how you answer the above questions, how would you rate your physical energy on a scale of 1 to 10?

AVAILABLE ENERGY

Based on the answer to the equation below, what is your available energy?

mental energy + emotional energy + physical energy ÷ 3 = ______

ENERGY GAP/SURPLUS

Based on the answer to the equation below, what is your energy gap or surplus?

available energy – required energy = energy gap or surplus

THE MESSAGE IN YOUR ENERGY GAP OR ENERGY SURPLUS

If the answer to this equation is a zero or a positive number, you have enough energy for the challenge. You may even have an energy surplus. If the answer is a negative number, you have an energy gap. In order to meet your challenge, you must either increase your energy or adjust your goal so that the required energy level is the same as or less than your available energy.

Keep in mind that your required energy and available energy are often in flux. There will be days when you have more energy and days when you have less. Pay attention to that so you can respond in real time and be resilient in the moment. There will be weeks when you have pushed hard, using more energy than usual. At some point you simply may not have enough energy to keep going because you've run through your reserves. Like me and Flo on that dreadful February day when the distance I drove drained my gas tank, you will find yourself out of gas. And like me, you may need to rally your resources when you realize you can't even open the gas tank without a little help! It's okay to call on those who can fill your emotional tank with encouragement, laughter, or a listening ear.

At other times, you'll find that you haven't just run out of energy at the end of a hard week, but you've adopted a lifestyle that is filled to capacity—overloaded, overwhelmed, and under resourced. You must make big changes to replenish your reserves and fill your energy tank in a sustainable way to support your vision and the challenges you must navigate to reach it.

How to Replenish Mental Energy

If you notice a gap between your vision and the cognitive energy needed to reach it, what will it take to consistently replenish your mental energy?

The first step is simply to be aware of how much energy cognitive tasks require. Then be intentional about caring for your mind. When you think nonstop, you must be intentional about giving your brain a break. That doesn't just mean stop thinking, although that is one form of rest. An important and counterintuitive form of rest is play.

Play activates a different part of your brain than rest. Play that involves physical activity has added benefits for your mental energy. Exercise boosts your memory and attention span. It increases blood flow to the brain and improves your focus and mood.[5] To boost mental energy, consider making these activities a habit:

- Walk briskly, jog, dance, and stretch.
- Play, engage in fun activities.

- Laugh and lighten up.
- Break projects into smaller tasks and reward yourself as you achieve them.
- Take regular breaks throughout the day, especially as you meet small goals.
- Take vacations and mental health days.
- Mark your wins with celebrations.
- Automate and delegate every decision that does not really require your input.

In addition, regularly run all your to-dos through a simple filter I call the Four D's:

- **Delegate it.** Make a habit of spending your mental energy on things only you can do. If someone else can effectively do or decide it, allow them to do so. That way, you do not expend energy unnecessarily.
- **Delay it.** Often, decisions and to-dos feel urgent when they are not. After all, our world is set up with instant communication and access to information. This can make it harder to decipher what is urgent and what isn't. Pause and prioritize. Everything doesn't have to get done right now. Some things can be done later. Know the difference.
- **Delete it.** Give yourself permission to drop tasks and activities from your to-do list that no longer make sense. You will immediately feel a sense of relief and reclaim some mental energy.
- **Do it.** Have you noticed a boost in your mental energy when you finally get something done that you've been procrastinating about? Productivity boosts your energy. When you get mental clarity about what deserves your mental energy and then spend your energy on it, you'll actually get a boost of dopamine. The practice of being intentional and consistent builds a powerful muscle of resilience.

RALLY YOUR MENTAL RESOURCES

Take your mental health and energy seriously. Continue to learn and grow, just as you are doing by reading this book right now. If you can, invest in a coach. Get therapy when you need it. Limit your intake of negative media influences, whether movies and television, news, or social media. And actively engage in a community of mentally healthy, purpose-focused people.

How to Replenish Emotional Energy

It seems counterintuitive that when you are faced with challenges and even negative circumstances, positive emotion is a strategy to help you conquer them. But it's true. The chemicals and hormones that are released into the brain and body when you experience positive emotions make you better able to withstand and overcome stress and challenges.[6] When you are in a positive state of mind, it broadens your scope of thinking, helping you see more options and think more creatively, leading to better decision-making and a better outlook. This, in turn, strengthens your relationships, ability to persevere, and desire to pursue higher goals. It also strengthens your immune system, making it less likely you'll get sick and more likely you'll live longer. Positive emotion is literally a success strategy.

Positive emotion is literally a success strategy.

Positive emotion builds over time like a cushion, softening the blow of adversity. When you've experienced abundant positive emotion, getting knocked off track by an unexpected challenge can feel like falling onto a mattress. If you've had excessive negative emotion for a long period, it can feel more like falling onto concrete with no padding to absorb some of the impact. So it is important to be intentional about cultivating positive emotion as an adaptive skill and preventive choice that puts you in a better position to handle unexpected adversity.

To improve your emotional energy, keep these things in mind:

- **Intentionally build positive emotion daily with simple habits.** For example, express gratitude and reflect on *why* you are grateful. We know that simply reflecting on the reason for your gratitude actually increases the amount of positive emotion you feel. Savor good moments. And build anticipation by noticing and creating something to look forward to. Positive anticipation is a happiness trigger.
- **Accept that it can take time and intention to undo the effects of negative emotions.** Have you ever noticed that you were still irritated when someone did something rude to you and then tried to make up for it by giving you a compliment or gift? That's because negative emotion is more powerful. It sticks. You probably recall your mistakes and failures more easily than your triumphs and good choices. And when you have had a series of tough challenges, it can take several wins before you feel confident and content again. Keep this in mind as you navigate challenges and negative encounters, especially in relationships. It can take time and intention to undo the effects of negative emotion.
- **Give yourself permission to feel negative emotions.** Cultivating positive emotions does not mean ignoring your negative ones. In fact, ignoring negative emotions can multiply them. They are a natural and healthy response to pain, disappointment, anger, and stress. Don't judge them as bad. Don't pretend you feel okay when you don't. It is what it is. When it comes to negative emotion, process it rather than suppress it. To process negative emotions, acknowledge what you feel. Accept your right to feel the way you feel. Make meaning out of your emotions by reflecting on the message behind them. Give yourself the space to feel what you feel, and seek support, a listening ear, time to heal or rest. Make a conscious choice not to allow your emotions to hijack your next steps; instead, pause and choose your response.

Once you've processed your negative emotions, you can clear space for positive emotions—such as hope, determination, and even gratitude—to emerge organically.

- **Recognize the major contribution you make to your own happiness.** According to the research of Dr. Sonja Lyubomirsky, author of *The How of Happiness*, we can think of the components of happiness as a "happiness pie." *Happiness is 50 percent genetic and 10 percent circumstantial, but the remaining 40 percent is due to intentional choices.*[7] There's nothing you can do about genetics. Circumstances are sometimes beyond your control, although preventive choices help you create the best possible scenarios. But 40 percent of your happiness is simply due to the choices you make daily. Acts of kindness and service, connecting with others, laughing, and playing help you cultivate positive emotion.

  Every day, do something to actively build positive emotion. Here are a few ideas:

  - Write down three things you are grateful for—and tell why.
  - Do something helpful or kind for someone else.
  - Connect through genuine conversation with no electronics or distractions.
  - Play. Do something just for fun and joy, not performance.
  - Turn your phone off; do nothing at all and savor it.

With positive emotional energy, it is much easier to practice adaptive skills like thought awareness and replacement and planning, as well as staying focused on your vision rather than getting distracted by your obstacles.

RALLY YOUR EMOTIONAL RESOURCES

Happiness and positive emotion are contagious—and so is negativity. Be selective about who you spend time with. Cultivate relationships with people whose attitude and outlook mirror what you aspire to—people who make you laugh, are forgiving, and have a positive attitude about life. If you are struggling and stuck in negative emotion, reach out for help. Talk to a wise friend or family member you trust. Join a support group of people dealing with similar challenges. Make an appointment with a therapist, clergyperson, or your health-care provider.

How to Replenish Physical Energy

To maintain or increase your physical energy, consider these areas:

- **Rest well.** When you get proper sleep, take breaks, and enjoy downtime, you'll be energized. To increase your available energy, get eight or more hours of sleep a night. Listen to your body. Take a nap if you're tired. And give yourself permission to do nothing on your days off. If that never happens on weekends, maybe it's time to take a day off just to rest.
- **Eat well.** A diet filled with fresh food—vegetables, fruits, nuts, and whole grains—can keep you feeling light and healthy. Heavy meals will weigh you down, so when you need extra energy, be intentional about what you eat. Be sure to drink plenty of water. Dehydration can cause you to feel tired, drain your energy, and lead to headaches and mental fatigue.
- **Move well.** Exercise is actually a happiness trigger. It releases endorphins and serotonin, causing a boost in your mood and even helping to ward off mild depression. Just twenty minutes of cardio movement will energize your mood for up to twenty-four hours. As you likely know, exercise has a host of physical benefits too.

RALLY YOUR PHYSICAL RESOURCES

Get annual physicals and seek medical care when something doesn't feel right. Don't delay because early detection of health problems can save your life, and at the very least, minimize the interruption that an illness can cause. Take fitness classes. If you can afford it, work with a trainer, nutritionist, or other specialist who can help you with specific goals. Use positive peer pressure by working out with others or setting joint goals and encouraging one another.

The Bigger the Challenge, the More Energy You Need

Your personal growth is the invisible key to closing the gap between where you are and where you really want to be, but your energy level is another often overlooked ingredient for resilience. We tend to underestimate what it really takes to conquer a challenge or achieve a vision. But if the required energy for your challenge is a level 10, you cannot overcome it with available energy at a level 5. Yet that is what so many of us attempt day after day. Doing so will frustrate you and even cause you to misdirect that frustration in ways that further deplete your energy. "Just push through" works sometimes, but if your strategy is to chronically push yourself to your limits, the reserve of energy you repeatedly tap into will eventually run dry. Suddenly burned out, you may find yourself giving up entirely and sabotaging your most authentic desires.

I drive an electric car now, but I have never forgotten the lesson I learned the day I ran out of gas a month after my sixteenth birthday. My car can go quite a long distance on a charge, but I recharge it overnight every night, determined never to run out of power. And just like my car, I am constantly refueling myself so I have the necessary energy available for the distance I must go to meet the demands of life and work.

So notice on a daily, weekly, and even annual basis whether you have an energy gap. Does your available energy meet or exceed the required energy level for your vision? If so, you are equipped to meet the challenge. If not, make a plan to close that gap—either by adjusting the goal so it requires less energy or by increasing your available energy level through intentional choices to boost your mental, emotional, and physical capacity.

Coach Yourself

- On a scale of 1 to 10, how much energy do you have available to accomplish your vision?
- On a scale of 1 to 10, what level of effort and energy does your vision require?
- What energizes you?
- What would you need to do daily and weekly to maintain the level of energy required for your vision?
- What gets in the way of incorporating those things into your life?
- How could you eliminate or minimize those obstacles?
- What experiment could you engage in to replenish your reserves and increase your energy level?
- When will you move forward with your experiment?

Try This

- ☐ Identify your energy gap.
- ☐ Decide what steps you will take to close it and when.
- ☐ Close that energy gap!

SAY IT WITH ME:

"I replenish my reserves to keep from burning out or giving up."

BONUS RULE

PAY IT FORWARD

How to apply the skills of resilience to help those around you

---

KEY MESSAGES

- You reach the fifth level of resilience when you pass on what you've learned.
- Meeting the needs of others will increase your own resilience.
- The only person who can decide how you should pay it forward is *you*.

This last rule is simple but meaningful: "Pay it forward."

Now that you've learned the ten rules of resilience that you can apply to any challenge you face, I'd like you to consider a bonus rule. It's focused not so much on how you can be resilient but rather on how you can spread resilience. Research tells us that happiness is contagious.[1] I believe resilience is too. Take what you've learned and help others become more resilient. Our world needs resilience more than ever before, and how you show up can have a ripple effect in your sphere of influence. Consider this often-told story that speaks to the significance of enabling greater resilience in others. It opens with a question asked during a lecture by the trailblazing cultural anthropologist Margaret Mead.

> "What is the earliest sign of civilization?" A clay pot? Iron? Tools? Agriculture? No, she claimed. To her, evidence of the earliest true civilization was a healed femur, a leg bone, which she held up before us in the lecture hall. She explained that

> such healings were never found in the remains of competitive, savage societies. There, clues of violence abounded: temples pierced by arrows, skulls crushed by clubs. But the healed femur showed that someone must have cared for the injured person—hunted on his behalf, brought him food, and served him at personal sacrifice.[2]

Being willing to help others weather their own adversity is a sign of compassion. I began this book by sharing the four levels of resilience. As you may recall, there are two levels below the line of resilience (malfunctioning and nonfunctioning) and two levels above the line (functioning and thriving). In any challenge, we may find ourselves on a sliding range between those four levels. Now I want to add a fifth level: paying it forward.

The fifth level of resilience belongs above thriving. At this stage, you have not only navigated your challenge resiliently, but you have healed, reflected, and gleaned the lessons of your experience so that you can use those lessons to support and encourage others to be resilient as they face their own challenges. You show compassion and empathy, inspire by example, share the wisdom of your experience, and give back in tangible ways.

With that in mind, I invite you to paint a vision of what this fifth level of resilience looks like for you. This part of your vision, and the resilience it requires, is *not* about you. It is about the impact you have on the resilience of *others*.

Ultimately, each of us has the potential to serve a greater purpose. That purpose is always about the impact we make on the world around us. Our world is increasingly stressful and disconnected, so many people lack the resilience skills that ideally would have been passed along while they were growing up. Others, who have weathered a constant barrage of adversities, may find themselves struggling to be resilient even though they once were.

Even before you reach a level of resilience that can be called thriving, your willingness to see the needs of others, and encourage or help them, can actually increase your resilience. That's because when you put your life into perspective, it makes it easier to choose thoughts that strengthen you. Dealing with your challenges requires a lot of self-focus. When you face difficulties, you can become hyperfocused on your problems and challenges. In fact, you can begin to ruminate on the situation to the point of creating anxiety or other issues. What you focus on expands. That means that your problems and challenges can take over your thought life and actions. One of the best things you can do is get your mind off yourself. By focusing on how you might serve someone else, you put your challenges into perspective as you realize that you are not the only person struggling. It moves you from the center of your focus and puts your life into perspective. Research shows that having a sense of service and purpose makes you happier by producing positive emotion, which strengthens your resilience.[3]

Additionally, if you have a tendency to make "upward social comparisons," where you determine how well you are doing only by observing people you perceive as doing much better than you, you will be less satisfied with life. Such comparisons decrease happiness and increase rates of anxiety and depression. If you have this habit, you can counteract it by noticing the plight of those not as fortunate. You can even choose to serve them in some way.

Resilience is built on adaptive skills, protective resources, and preventive measures, but each of these must be more intentionally cultivated than ever before. Protective resources such as close family ties and friendships, as well as the safety nets of financial savings and strong community, have declined. Americans have smaller families, live farther away from relatives, have fewer close friendships, and are less likely to participate in worship services and a faith community than they did several decades ago. Many people also have less financial security because of increased debt, decreased savings, and the high costs of education and housing.

To pay it forward you must reach back and glean the wisdom of your resilience. Rather than glossing over the times you used your resilience to achieve your goal, you reflect on a time when you were at your best. One way this can be done is through appreciative inquiry, a system developed by business professor David Cooperrider.[4] As part of this approach, think of a success you've had and ask yourself, *What enabled that?* By answering that question, you intentionally recreate what enabled you to do your best. Then, when you encounter someone to whom you want to pay it forward, you can pass on the lessons you gained from your own experience. As you consider that success, reflect on these pillars, which may reveal more wisdom that you can share with others:

Adaptive skills: What were the thoughts that threatened to keep you stuck, and how did you change them? What's your biggest lesson in making that shift to thoughts that strengthen you?

Protective resources: What were the protective resources that mattered most in helping you to be resilient in the face of this challenge? What is the message or lesson that you learned from tapping your protective resources that you want to share with others?

Preventive measures: As a result of going through this challenge, what preventive measures did you implement so that you're better equipped to deal with a similar challenge or minimize the likelihood of dealing with the same challenge again?

When you can notice and name what enabled you to do your best, you're able to share it with others.

Adaptive skills such as thought awareness, planning, and decision-making are made easier by mindfulness—being fully present. To be aware of your thoughts and remain intentional as you move through the five stages of success to tackle a challenge (see pages 71–75), you need mindfulness and energy. However, the onslaught of technology vying for your attention is relentless, and attention spans have shortened in recent decades.

That means that even when we do connect with others, our mode of communication has shifted from face-to-face gatherings and phone conversations to isolated text messages, group chats, and social media posts. Our media content is customized but isolating. That can be particularly problematic for those who have few protective resources or opportunities to take preventive measures.

So, much like the student who asked Margaret Mead to identify the first sign of civilization, I once asked Dr. Martin Seligman during class, "We are studying human flourishing and happiness. What is the application of positive psychology in an underserved, disadvantaged community where there is little flourishing but instead economic struggle, unstable family dynamics, and crime?"

Without missing a beat, Dr. Seligman said that the key is to study those who somehow find a way to thrive despite the odds. What was different about them and their situation that enabled them to rise above their circumstances and empowered them to thrive? Study that, then use those stories to find solutions and teach others to do the same. Paying it forward is not only about sharing your story but also about passing on the wisdom you gain through observation.

One of my favorite coaching questions is one I stumbled upon while working with a new client nearly twenty years ago as she was struggling to articulate her life's purpose: *How is someone's life better because they cross paths with you?*

The client, who had spent a couple of years fruitlessly trying to figure out how to sum up her purpose succinctly, effortlessly responded with a one-sentence description of her purpose. She was amazed, and so was I. I've been sharing the question ever since. What is your answer to that question?

ASK YOURSELF

How is someone's life better because they cross paths with you?

Purpose often emerges from pain. Your suffering can range from discomfort to devastation. And when you are resilient, your recovery is a journey that offers an opportunity to get better, stronger, and wiser. Whatever challenges you endure, a sure sign of your resilience is when you get to the point where you begin to ask, "How can I make a difference with this newfound wisdom I've gained?"

My purpose of inspiring people to live more fulfilling lives emerged from that early season in my career when I hadn't stepped into the kind of work I really wanted to do. I also didn't listen to or honor my authentic self in relationships. I played it small and paid a price. Yet the journey has shaped me in good ways.

When Chaunté Lowe was at a low point in her cancer journey, losing her physical strength but fighting through chemo treatment, she says, "Breast cancer made others more visible to me. My eyes became open to others facing similar experiences."

I can relate, as I often said something similar after the humbling and devastating experience of a divorce. On the other side of it, I felt others' pain more deeply. It made me a more compassionate person. It's not that I didn't have compassion before that; it's just that when something rocks the foundation of your identity and your everyday life so completely, you suddenly see everything differently. Pain and fear, if you allow it, strip away any pretense or illusions of the superficial. In their place, once the fog has burned away, you see the human experience more clearly.

"I took the lesson that I was learning, and I wanted to reach back and help other people," Chaunté says. She started by posting online, writing about her hair falling out and then losing her fingernails. She decided that in every post, not only would she be authentic about what she was going through, but also she would share hope. "People don't just need to see your hard moments; they need to see that, yes, it was hard, but there is hope!" she notes. "I was very vulnerable and transparent with what I was going through."

Not long after Chaunté became cancer-free, the pandemic hit. As a former Olympian and cancer survivor who had shared so openly on social media about her journey, Chaunté began getting invitations to speak at virtual events. "I felt it was important to take my lessons as an athlete and cancer survivor and package them up to give to the next person," she says. She saw it as a gift to help others get through challenges, whether breast cancer or divorce or foreclosure.

When I think of my own strong convictions around resilience, I think of the seeds that were planted by those who came before me, including my maternal great-grandfather, "Daddy Joe." He died when my mother was just eleven, but I have his picture hanging in our home. Joe Greenlee was born in South Carolina in 1898 and taught his children, including my grandmother, Mama Pearl, the importance of business ownership as a means of claiming independence and dignity during the Jim Crow era. He somehow managed to own a thriving business in the downtown district of my parents' hometown, and in a time of fierce segregation, he served many loyal customers, both black and white. His was the only such business in the area. Three of his four daughters went into business for themselves. Each time my mother talked about Daddy Joe when I was a kid, it gave me a greater sense of self and of the convictions and resilience we come from, and it sparked my interest in having a business of my own.

Similarly, my paternal grandparents shared an abundance of wisdom despite their limited formal education. My grandfather died when I was nine and my grandmother when I was eleven, but I spent every summer of my young childhood with them. They experienced tyranny and injustice but were kind and generous to everyone they encountered. I remember Grandaddy sharing with me once that after his father disappeared when he was in the fifth grade, he dropped out of school to help the family earn money. There were days, he said, when all he ate was an apple off someone else's tree. That explained why my grandparents wasted nothing, managed their resources so well, and helped others. They shared their stories of growing up in the rural South as sharecroppers during the Great Depression. It was hard work and an honest, meager living. But when I was about nine, my grandmother told me that after being cheated out of their earnings one year, they gave it up. My grandaddy had been so furious about being cheated again at the end of the year that he stormed into the house to get his shotgun so he could confront the landowner. Grandmama begged him to calm down, knowing that if he did, he'd end up dead and hanging from a tree. That was their reality.

After that, my grandparents decided to make a change so they could have better control over their lives. They controlled the controllable by moving from the country in rural Iva, South Carolina, to the county seat, Anderson. Grandaddy got a job at a textile mill, where he did heavy manual work outside with other black men until the company finally desegregated in the 1960s and they gained the right to work inside the factory. Grandmama worked as a domestic, cleaning and taking care of children for a local doctor. Both worked hard and eventually got better jobs. They raised not only my father but also multiple nieces and nephews as their own. They bought a home, nurtured their children, and did well for themselves. When one of my cousins asked Grandaddy if we were rich, I remember he said, "We're not rich; we're just well-a-do's." It was his country way of saying we were doing well.

This sense of belonging to a bigger story and deciding how to carry that story forward was instilled in me at a young age through the power of my family's history. It was often shared casually while sitting under my grandparents' backyard apple tree on summer afternoons while I was stringing green beans or shucking corn with them. It was shared by my parents at the dinner table or during car rides, when my mother told me about her unpleasant experience as one of the first students to integrate her high school. My father talked about the tight-knit, segregated community he grew up in, as well as the lessons Grandaddy taught him about hard work, not making excuses, and building something that gives your children a better start than you had.

I was impacted, not just by their stories, but by my observations of how they handled challenges—from my grandparents' kindness and love despite all the injustice they'd faced to my father's loss of both parents and his brother by the age of thirty-three to my mother's fight to recover from and adapt to disabilities and loss. Their resilience through circumstances and disadvantages I didn't face gave me a sense of responsibility to take full advantage of what they hadn't had access to. It made me want to build on their foundation.

To this day, when I feel discouraged, their history puts my challenges into perspective. *If they got through that, I can get through this.* They all paid it forward, and I am inspired to pay it forward too—not just to my children and younger family members but to my team members, neighbors, community, and every person who encounters the words I write and speak. When you pay it forward, you offer perspective, hope, and wisdom to another. But you also help yourself.

What about you?

Paying It Forward

WHO DO YOU WANT TO IMPACT?

You have a sphere of influence. Decide the type of positive impact you want to have on those around you, and then set out to influence them. Perhaps there are certain groups you can target—those whose circumstances reflect your area of purpose and passion or who have a point of connection with you. If you've had patterns of dysfunction in the past, paying it forward might mean you begin showing up differently in the relationship. You can break the cycle. You can control your words and actions and shift the dynamic. If other relationships have been functional but not intentional, you can share your wisdom and care. Decide who you want to pay it forward to.

WHAT DO YOU WANT TO PAY FORWARD?

You might want to teach your favorite rules of resilience within your family or your teams. You might make it a habit to discuss which rules of resilience you employ when you face specific challenges. You can share authentic lessons from your successes and your failures. Your willingness to see yourself as part of a bigger solution is critical.

There are four ways to plant seeds that pay it forward.

- **Compassion: Empathize.** Compassion is sensitivity to the mental, emotional, and physical suffering of others and a desire to relieve or ease that suffering when possible. Remember what it was like when you were in a similar situation—how it felt and what was so hard about it. Doing so will give you direction in terms of how to encourage and support others through their adversity.
- **Inspiration: Serve as a resilience role model.** Early in my coaching career, I had a great coach named Michele. One day when I was discussing a project I wanted to use to inspire people, she told me, "You *are* inspiration." At first, I didn't understand, but her words soon shifted my perspective. She explained that by living and working in a way that reflected my values, I would inspire and encourage those clients who were seeking to better align their lives with their own values. The same is true for you. Those in your sphere of influence can be inspired to show up more resiliently and powerfully because they have observed you doing so in the face of challenges—perhaps imperfectly, but with consistency.
- **Wisdom: Share your lessons.** Pinpoint the lessons you've learned and the rules of resilience you've used to overcome challenges. Share them when others are looking for feedback, support, or planning. After Michelle Williams navigated her way back to mental health, she found a new passion for raising awareness about mental health and wellness. She wrote a book, *Checking In*, and decided to host a podcast with the same name. She began speaking, completed coach training at The CaPP Institute, and became a Certified Personal and Executive Coach, adding the ability to coach people to her skill set, all while performing on Broadway. She wanted to help others create breakthroughs to move them from where they are to where they really want to be while navigating the obstacles along the way. Remember, purpose can emerge from painful circumstances. You've reached the highest level of resilience when you're not just thriving but supporting and sharing the skills and lessons of resilience to others.

- **Action: Pay it forward tangibly.** The last way to pay it forward is to give back in tangible ways, whether by mentoring, volunteering, or simply providing valuable information or introductions. You may provide access to protective resources such as money, education, training, time, and connections. Access to any of these may enable someone else to be more resilient. Think of the people or particular group you are particularly passionate about helping or a cause dear to your heart.

Consider how others helped you be more resilient by sharing their lessons, empathizing or inspiring you, or giving you tangible resources that enabled you to navigate your challenge. How might you do something similar for someone else? My experience as a nineteen-year-old student navigating a messy college journey with the help of a college staff member whose name I don't even know was pivotal in my life. Being given a second chance and scholarship after a failed first year at a different university has influenced how I give charitably. It has led me to support scholarship funds for nontraditional students and those who stand out for their leadership, responsibility, or resilience—not just their academics. I know what it's like to piece together a college experience and to be creative in finding ways to fund college without an impressive transcript but with the ability and drive to do impactful work. All I needed was for the right person to be willing to listen to my story.

What is a cause that tugs at your heart? Think of your own past adversities or challenges and identify an experience where someone gave you a helping hand or a boost through their guidance, resources, or access to resources, helping you to be resilient and navigate your challenge successfully. Decide how you want to pay it forward.

Resilience isn't just needed for us on an individual level; it is also needed to cope with the challenges and stressors in the greater world around us. Think about the people, causes, and issues closest to your heart. How you show up impacts how those around you show up. It helps you reach the goal or overcome the challenge. But a bigger question is, How will your resilience serve others? It can have a ripple effect in your closest relationships, your family, your workplace, your community, and the world.

You pay it forward when someone faces a challenge and draws inspiration, wisdom, and confidence from your resilience. This type of contagiousness spreads through families, workplaces, and cultures. It is the power of seeing someone model what it looks like to pivot and adapt, to forgive and move on, and to make intentional choices that set you up for success rather than failure. Sometimes all someone needs in order to show up differently is to see that it can be done.

As you practice the rules of resilience and notice how these skills and tools transform the way you face challenges, don't keep what you learn to yourself. Teach those lessons. Share them.

In your family, what do you want to teach the next generation through your actions?

At work, how could you model and advocate for a culture of resilience and well-being, two traits that foster productivity and excellence?

In your community, how could you cultivate connections that build bridges rather than divides?

You don't need to pay it forward from a stage as a speaker or from the page as a writer. You can do so in volunteer work or everyday conversations around the dinner table or over lunch.

Let your children see you grow. Let them see you make mistakes, admit them, and then grow into a better, wiser, stronger version of yourself. In the workplace, introduce the concept of resilience as a necessary skill set among team members in order for an organization—and everyone in it—to thrive. Let your coworkers and team members see you lead with authenticity, adapt gracefully to change, and close your energy and growth gaps to achieve your potential. In your community, be compassionate and kind. Look people in the eye. Slow down and connect. Be intentional about how you show up.

Talk with others about the rules of resilience that resonate most with you. Help others see that if you can do it, they can too. Never underestimate the ripple effect that resilience can make in your closest relationships, your family, your workplace, your community, and the world.

Coach Yourself

- ► In what way(s) have you been resilient in the last year? What challenge have you overcome?
- ► In what way(s) have you been hyperfocused on a problem or challenge?
- ► In what way(s) has this challenge made you wiser, stronger, or more compassionate?
- ► Whom could you impact with that newfound wisdom, strength, or compassion—and how might they benefit from that?
- ► What step will you take this month to serve others? How do you hope it might expand your purpose or shift your perspective?

Try This

- ☐ Remind yourself of your purpose.
- ☐ Look for the purpose in painful circumstances and the message in the mess.
- ☐ Act on that purpose.
- ☐ Identify who or where you can serve, then give back and make an impact with your compassion, inspiration, wisdom, or acts of service.
- ☐ Reflect on the perspective shift that occurs when you pay it forward.

SAY IT WITH ME:

"When I focus on serving others,
I strengthen my purpose and perspective."

EPILOGUE

RULES AS TOOLS

Rules sometimes get a bad rap.

And I get it. After all, resilience requires flexibility and creative thinking, and we tend to think of rules as rigid and confining. However, now that you've reached the end of this book, you no doubt realize that the ten rules of resilience don't provide prescriptions for every situation you will face. Instead, they are principles that are generally true for everyone but that you will want to apply and adapt to your own circumstances. For example, while it's true that we all need to expect the unexpected (Resilience Rule #1), your response—how you plan for, think about, and respond to unanticipated challenges and opportunities—may look different from the approach others take.

So where do you go from here?

Whenever you're perplexed by an unexpected challenge or opportunity, I encourage you to see this book as a resource you can come back to. Review the list of rules and key messages on pages 229–230. Once you've identified the rule or related step that speaks to the problem you're encountering, you may want to go back to that chapter and work through the self-coaching questions and exercises. When you engage with them thoughtfully and honestly, you may discover the direction, answers, and action steps you need.

Even when life seems to be going well, continue to build your adaptive skills, protective resources, and preventive measures. (For a refresher on these three pillars, turn to pages 9–12.) As you strive to become a more positive, balanced, and self-disciplined person; as you get better at managing your finances, looking for learning opportunities, and nurturing your relationships; and as you plan for the known and unknown challenges ahead, you will naturally become a more resilient person. Not only that, but you'll be ready to pass on your wisdom and experience to those who you are open to and may benefit from them.

These rules, then, aren't meant to be ends in themselves; instead, they are tools you can wield whenever you find yourself in a tight spot or are ready to build something new. Greater resilience, after all, isn't your ultimate goal in life, but it's a vital instrument on your way there.

RULES OF RESILIENCE

Resilience Rule #1: "Expect the unexpected"

- Don't just think positively, think accurately.
- Accept that changes and challenges are part of life.
- Look for ways to strengthen your pillars so you're ready for unexpected opportunities.

Resilience Rule #2: "Choose thoughts that strengthen you"

- It's not what happens that matters most; it's how you think about what happens.
- You can self-coach your way to more helpful interpretations of stressful events.
- With practice, you can rewire the patterns in your brain for greater resilience.

Resilience Rule #3: "Focus on the vision, not the obstacle"

- Focus on the vision; work around the obstacle.
- Create your Vision Manifesto and use it as a tool to get unstuck.
- Knowing the five stages of success will enhance your patience, endurance, and results.

Resilience Rule #4: "Control the controllable; accept the rest"

- Accept responsibility so you can move from a passive mentality to a proactive one.
- Learn to operate from an internal locus of control.
- Decide to be "better, not bitter" on the other side of your challenge.

Resilience Rule #5: "Rally your resources"

- Personal resources make resilience easier, so assess and build the right ones.
- Strong relationships are a foundational resource for your personal resilience.
- Be willing to ask for help.

Resilience Rule #6: "Close your growth gap"

- Performance goals are your vision; growth goals are the engine.
- A growth mindset builds humility and resilience, but a fixed mindset does the opposite.
- Taking action is the key to growth.

Resilience Rule #7: "Don't pretend, don't defend"

- Pretending prolongs a problem; admitting it gives you permission to fix it.
- Give yourself permission to be imperfect.
- Use failure to analyze, not penalize.

Resilience Rule #8: "Find the opportunity in the challenge"

- Intentionally embrace a specific type of optimism that predicts success and resilience.
- Anticipate and cultivate post-traumatic growth.
- "Constructive interpretations" can transform your challenges into opportunities.

Resilience Rule #9: "Know when to grit, know when to quit"

- Resilience is more than just perseverance; it's the wisdom to know when to quit.
- Grit also requires grace.
- Purpose fuels perseverance, so get clear about yours.

Resilience Rule #10: "Close your energy gap"

- Your energy level must match the level of your vision, or you'll burn out.
- Self-care and self-compassion are critical energy boosters.
- Negative is more powerful than positive, so carefully cultivate the positive.

Bonus Rule: "Pay it forward"

- You reach the fifth level of resilience when you pass on what you've learned.
- Meeting the needs of others will increase your own resilience.
- The only person who can decide how you should pay it forward is *you*.

ACKNOWLEDGMENTS

Thank you to the people who encouraged me and enabled this book to become reality. I indeed rallied my resources to bring it to life, and I could not have done it alone. I extend my deepest gratitude to . . .

My supportive and enthusiastic husband, Jeff. Thank you for always believing in me, being so proud of me, and encouraging my ideas without hesitation. And thank you to our children, Alex, Addie, and Sophie—not only are you resilient, but your presence in my life has taught me so much and made me better, stronger, and wiser. I love you.

Andrea Heinecke, my literary agent. Thank you for your longstanding guidance, efforts, and belief in my work.

Jan Long Harris and Jillian Schlossberg, thank you for the opportunity to work with you and the incredible team at Tyndale.

Kim Miller, my editor at Tyndale, and Annette Hayward and the copyediting team, thank you for your tireless and meticulous effort on the editing of this book. I appreciate you.

Margot Starbuck, my personal editor, thank you for your spirited and speedy editing and helping me get ideas out of my head and onto the page.

Everyone involved in the creation of the cover—Libby Dykstra, Lindsey Bergsma, Kaylee Small, and Dean Renninger of Tyndale; my photographer Michele Mabie and my visual brand manager Caleb London—for your thorough, energetic, and creative work.

Mark Cole, CEO of Maxwell Leadership. Thank you for your friendship and encouragement over the last two decades, your invitation to lead the coach training effort for more than 50,000 Maxwell Leadership Certified Team members around the globe, and your belief in this book. Thank you for connecting me and John in a shared passion for the power of personal growth and strong leadership.

John Maxwell, the world's most prolific author on leadership and my mentor. Thank you for your example, your guidance, the gift of your time—and especially for writing the powerful foreword to this book!

Inspire Inc. team—Tonya Beaty, Taylor Hendrix, Caleb London, Alena Marie, Alexis Murray, Leone Murray, Wade Murray, and Kristen Terlitsky. What a gift to work with each of you. Thank you for your support of this book. And Caleb, thank you especially for our engaging discussions about these rules as I developed them, and your feedback and positive energy that encouraged me to keep going!

The team at Maxwell Leadership, including the marketing team of Jake Decker, Jared Cagle, Taylor Melton, and Jessica Duquette. To Chris Robinson, thank you for your positive energy and welcoming spirit. I love being a "match" for the Maxwell Leadership Certified Team members. And to the Corporate Solutions Group, led by Chris Goede along with Perry Holley, Tammy Grabowski and Sara Henderson, with whom I have created the resilience training curriculum for organizations, rooted in the principles from *Rules of Resilience*.

My mom, Leone Adger Murray, and my dad, John Burton. Thank you for modeling resilience for me, for the lessons you've taught me, and for your unwavering support and encouragement my whole life. I owe much of my resilience to your influence.

The three friends whose stories I share in these pages, T. Michelle Williams, Tara-Leigh Cobble, and Chaunté Lowe. Thank you for allowing me to interview you and share your resilience and wisdom with my readers.

Last but not least, my former positive psychology professors at the University of Pennsylvania, especially Dr. Martin E. P. Seligman, Dr. James Pawelski, Dr. Karen Reivich, Dr. Angela Duckworth, and the late Dr. Christopher Peterson. Your work transformed my life and work, and I am forever grateful to have had the opportunity to learn from you.

And to you reading this, thank you for spending time with my words. My hope is that this message has made you better, wiser, and stronger.

NOTES

INTRODUCTION

1. I am such a believer in the power of coaching that I am one of just over 4 percent of credentialed coaches worldwide who have achieved the Master Certified Coach accreditation through the International Coaching Federation, which provides rigorous, independent certification to coaching professionals.
2. "Psychological Capital: What It Is and Why Employers Need It Now," American Psychological Association, August 21, 2023, https://www.apa.org/topics/healthy-workplaces/psychological-capital.

CREATE AND CULTIVATE A PERSONAL SYSTEM OF RESILIENCE

1. "Resilience," American Psychological Association, accessed December 30, 2024, https://www.apa.org/topics/resilience.
2. "Supportive Relationships and Active Skill-Building Strengthen the Foundations of Resilience," National Scientific Council on the Developing Child, Working Paper 13 (Center on the Developing Child, Harvard University, May 28, 2015), https://developingchild.harvard.edu/wp-content/uploads/2024/10/The-Science-of-Resilience2.pdf.
3. "Use of Trivalent Influenza Vaccines for the 2024–2025 US Influenza Season," US Food and Drug Administration, accessed December 30, 2024, https://www.fda.gov/vaccines-blood-biologics/lot-release/use-trivalent-influenza-vaccines-2024-2025-us-influenza-season.
4. John Elflein, "Number of Influenza Deaths in the United States from 2010 to 2023," Statista, March 28, 2024, https://www.fda.gov/vaccines-blood-biologics/lot-release/use-trivalent-influenza-vaccines-2024-2025-us-influenza-season.
5. When the Harvard Center on the Developing Child explored how key life skills are passed on to children, they identified resilience as a primary driver of children's well-being. For more, see National Scientific Council on the Developing Child, "Supportive Relationships and Active Skill-Building."

6. National Scientific Council on the Developing Child, "Supportive Relationships and Active Skill-Building."
7. Michele M. Tugade et al., "Psychological Resilience and Positive Emotional Granularity: Examining the Benefits of Positive Emotions on Coping and Health," *Journal of Personality* 72, no. 6 (December 2004): 1161–1190, https://doi.org/10.1111/j.1467-6494.2004.00294.x; David L. Roth et al., "Religious Involvement and Health over Time: Predictive Effects in a National Sample of African Americans," *Journal for the Scientific Study of Religion* 55, no. 2 (June 2016): 417–424, https://doi.org/10.1111/jssr.12269.

RESILIENCE RULE #1: EXPECT THE UNEXPECTED

1. Blake Stilwell, "The Real-Life Murphy and How 'Murphy's Law' Came to Be," Military.com, June 10, 2022, https://www.military.com/history/real-life-murphy-and-how-murphys-law-came-be.html.
2. Eric Lagatta, "Lotto Regret: Pitfalls of Powerball, Lottery Winners Serve as Cautionary Tales as Jackpots Swell," *USA Today*, updated July 20, 2023, https://www.usatoday.com/story/news/nation/2023/07/19/powerball-mega-millions-winners-instant-billionaire-regrets/70430571007/.
3. Ed Flynn, "Bankruptcy Grab Bag of Fun Facts," *ABI Journal*, December 2015, https://abi.org/abi-journal/bankruptcy-grab-bag-of-fun-facts.
4. Hannah Dailey, "Ariana Grande Announces 'The Boy Is Mine' Remix Featuring Brandy & Monica: 'Cannot Believe This Is Real,'" *Billboard*, June 17, 2024, https://www.billboard.com/music/music-news/ariana-grande-brandy-monica-the-boy-is-mine-remix-announced-1235711231/.

RESILIENCE RULE #2: CHOOSE THOUGHTS THAT STRENGTHEN YOU

1. Einat Levy-Gigi and Simone Shamay-Tsoory, "Affect Labeling: The Role of Timing and Intensity," *PLoS One* 17, no. 12 (December 29, 2022): e0279303, https://doi.org/10.1371/journal.pone.0279303.
2. NKJV.
3. Judith S. Beck and Sarah Fleming, "A Brief History of Aaron T. Beck, MD, and Cognitive Behavior Therapy," *Clinical Psychology in Europe* 3, no. 2 (June 18, 2021); e6701, https://doi.org/10.32872/cpe.6701.
4. "Dr. Aaron T. Beck: A Life Well-Lived," Beck Institute, accessed December 31, 2024, https://beckinstitute.org/about/dr-aaron-t-beck.
5. In the past, I called this framework TTR for "Trigger, Thoughts, Reactions" but have chosen to rename it STR for "Stressor, Thoughts, Reactions" because *stressor* is more accurate, and the word *trigger* has some negative associations I do not want to evoke.
6. "Triple-Negative Breast Cancer," American Cancer Society, accessed December 31, 2024, https://www.cancer.org/cancer/types/breast-cancer/about/types-of-breast-cancer/triple-negative.html.

7. Valorie Burton, host, *Coaching and Positive Psychology*, podcast, episode 13, "The Neuroscience of Getting Unstuck: A Conversation with Dr. Ebony Glover," The CaPP Institute, April 26, 2022.

RESILIENCE RULE #3: FOCUS ON THE VISION, NOT THE OBSTACLE

1. Jerry Jenkins, "Book Rejections: 3 Ways to Go from Rejection to Success" (blog post), August 5, 2024, https://jerryjenkins.com/book-rejections/.
2. This book, *Jeff Herman's Guide to Book Publishers, Editors and Literary Agents*, is currently in its twenty-ninth edition (Novato, CA: New World Library, 2023).
3. I self-published *Rich Minds, Rich Rewards* in 1999. The Villard imprint of Random House released it under the same title in 2001.
4. C. R. Snyder et al., "Hope Theory, Measurements, and Applications to School Psychology," *School Psychology Quarterly* 18, no. 2 (2003): 122–139, https://doi.org/10.1521/scpq.18.2.122.21854.
5. Tanya Tucker, vocalist, "Strong Enough to Bend," by Beth Nielsen Chapman and Don Schlitz, produced by Jerry Crutchfield, Capitol Records, released as a single in 1988.
6. "About the Podcast," *The Bible Recap*, accessed on December 9, 2024, https://www.thebiblerecap.com/about.
7. Paula M. Loveday et al., "The Best Possible Selves Intervention: A Review of the Literature to Evaluate Efficacy and Guide Future Research," *Journal of Happiness Studies* 19, no. 2 (February 2018), https://doi.org/10.1007/s10902-016-9824-z; Laura A. King, "The Health Benefits of Writing about Life Goals," *Personality and Social Psychology Bulletin* 27, no. 7 (July 2001): 798–807, https://doi.org/10.1177/0146167201277003.
8. King, "The Health Benefits of Writing about Life Goals."
9. Visit https://brave.valorieburton.com/optin-vision-manifesto1679335025071.

RESILIENCE RULE #4: CONTROL THE CONTROLLABLE; ACCEPT THE REST

1. American psychologist Julian B. Rotter developed this concept in the mid-twentieth century. See Julian B. Rotter, "Generalized Expectancies for Internal versus External Control of Reinforcement," *Psychological Monographs* 80, no. 1 (1966): 1–28, https://doi.org/10.1037/h0092976.
2. Hielke Buddelmeyer and Nattavudh Powdthavee, "Can Having Internal Locus of Control Insure Against Negative Shocks? Psychological Evidence from Panel Data," *Journal of Economic Behavior and Organization* 122 (February 2016): 88–109. https://doi.org/10.1016/j.jebo.2015.11.014.
3. "Statistics and Facts," Brain Aneurysm Foundation, accessed January 2, 2025, https://www.bafound.org/statistics-and-facts/.
4. "Know the Facts on Brain Aneurysms," https://lisafoundation.org/know-the-facts/; "Brain Aneurysm," Cleveland Clinic, updated February 10, 2023, https://my.clevelandclinic.org/health/diseases/16800-brain-aneurysm.

5. Steven F. Maier and Martin E. P. Seligman, "Learned Helplessness: Theory and Evidence," *Journal of Experimental Psychology: General* 105, no. 1 (1976): 3–46. https://ppc.sas.upenn.edu/sites/default/files/lhtheoryevidence.pdf.
6. *APA Dictionary of Psychology*, "Learned Helplessness," updated April 19, 2018, https://dictionary.apa.org/learned-helplessness.

RESILIENCE RULE #5: RALLY YOUR RESOURCES

1. Fatih Ozbay et al., "Social Support and Resilience to Stress: From Neurobiology to Clinical Practice," *Psychiatry (Edgmont)* 4, no. 5 (May 2007): 35–40, https://pmc.ncbi.nlm.nih.gov/articles/PMC2921311/; Ye Cui, "Goal-Setting Theory," *Theoretical Models for Teaching and Research*, accessed January 6, 2025, https://opentext.wsu.edu/theoreticalmodelsforteachingandresearch/chapter/goal-setting-theory/.
2. Michelle Williams, *Checking In: How Getting Real about Depression Saved My Life—and Can Save Yours* (Nashville: Thomas Nelson, 2021).
3. Ozbay, "Social Support and Resilience to Stress."
4. Cindy Lamothe and Crystal Raypole, "Is Your Relationship Toxic? Signs and How to Cope," Healthline, updated February 7, 2024, https://www.healthline.com/health/toxic-relationship.
5. Mark A. Bellis et al., "Does Continuous Trusted Adult Support in Childhood Impart Life-Course Resilience against Adverse Childhood Experiences—A Retrospective Study on Adult Health-Harming Behaviours and Mental Well-Being," *BMC Psychiatry* 17, no. 1 (March 23, 2017): 110, https://pmc.ncbi.nlm.nih.gov/articles/PMC5364707/.
6. "InBrief: The Science of Resilience," Harvard University Center on the Developing Child," May 20, 2015, https://developingchild.harvard.edu/wp-content/uploads/2024/10/InBrief-The-Science-of-Resilience-1.pdf.

RESILIENCE RULE #6: CLOSE YOUR GROWTH GAP

1. Terry Gaspard, "10 Rules for a Successful Second Marriage," The Gottman Institute, September 23, 2016, https://www.gottman.com/blog/10-rules-successful-second-marriage/.
2. John C. Maxwell, "The Law of the Lid," chap. 1 in *The 21 Irrefutable Laws of Leadership: Follow Them and People Will Follow You*, anniversary ed. (HarperCollins, 2007), 1–10.
3. Carol S. Dweck, *Mindset: The New Psychology of Success* (New York: Ballantine Books, 2007), 3.

RESILIENCE RULE #7: DON'T PRETEND, DON'T DEFEND

1. The cause of the tragic collision near Reagan International Airport between a passenger jet and a military helicopter in January 2025 was still under investigation at the time of this book's publication. Preliminary

evidence, however, found no evidence of airline pilot error. See Elizabeth Chuck, Jon Schuppe, and Melissa Chan, "What Caused the Deadly Midair Collision Between a Passenger Jet and an Army Helicopter?" NBC News, January 30, 2025, https://www.nbcnews.com/news/us-news/washington-dc-plane-crash-helicopter-cause-investigation-rcna189975.

2. Ben Cohen, "Flying in America Has Actually Never Been Safer," *Wall Street Journal*, January 12, 2024, https://www.wsj.com/business/airlines/plane-safety-airlines-boeing-never-been-safer-adbe2453; Peter Dizikes, "Study: Flying Keeps Getting Safer," Massachusetts Institute of Technology news release, August 7, 2024, https://news.mit.edu/2024/study-flying-keeps-getting-safer-0807.
3. "Aviation Safety Action Program," Federal Aviation Administration, updated December 17, 2024, https://www.faa.gov/about/initiatives/asap.
4. Ken Kaye, "Mysterious Aviation Disasters Help Set a Deadly Record in 1996," *Washington Post*, December 31, 1996, https://www.washingtonpost.com/archive/politics/1996/12/31/mysterious-aviation-disasters-help-set-a-deadly-record-in-1996/f1a9d8fe-bf61-438d-949d-822aca893de7/
5. Matthew L. Wald, "Fatal Crashes of Airplanes Decline 65% in U.S.," *New York Times*, September 30, 2007, https://www.nytimes.com/2007/10/01/business/worldbusiness/01iht-01safety.7693141.html.
6. Andy Pasztor, "The Airline Safety Revolution," *Wall Street Journal*, April 16, 2021, https://www.wsj.com/articles/the-airline-safety-revolution-11618585543.
7. James W. Pennebaker et al., "Disclosure of Traumas and Immune Function: Health Implications for Psychotherapy," *Journal of Consulting and Clinical Psychology* 56, no. 2 (1988): 239–245, https://doi.org/10.1037/0022-006x.56.2.239.
8. Monika Eckstein et al., "Calming Effects of Touch in Human, Animal, and Robotic Interaction—Scientific State-of-the-Art and Technical Advances," *Frontiers in Psychiatry* 11 (November 3, 2020): 555058, httsp://doi.org/10.3389/fpsyt.2020.555058.
9. Kristin Neff, "The Physiology of Self-Compassion," *Psychology Today*, July 2, 2012, https://www.psychologytoday.com/us/blog/the-power-self-compassion/201207/the-physiology-self-compassion.
10. Jan Vymětal, "Authenticity in Psychology and Psychotherapy" [in Czech], *Sborník Lékařský* 103, no. 3 (2002): 313–321, https://pubmed.ncbi.nlm.nih.gov/12688175.
11. Tony Schwartz, "The Importance of Naming Your Emotions," *New York Times*, April 3, 2015, https://www.nytimes.com/2015/04/04/business/dealbook/the-importance-of-naming-your-emotions.html.
12. Richard E. Watts, "Reflecting 'As If,'" *Counseling Today*, April 2013, https://www.counseling.org/publications/counseling-today-magazine/article-archive/article/legacy/reflecting-as-if.

RESILIENCE RULE #8: FIND THE OPPORTUNITY IN THE CHALLENGE

1. Scott Craven, "You Won't Believe Where McDonald's Opened Its First Drive-Thru," *Arizona Republic*, August 29, 2016, https://www.azcentral.com/story/travel/arizona/2016/08/29/mcdonalds-first-drive-through-sierra-vista-arizona/88009974/; "The First McDonald's Drive Thru Was Inspired by U.S. Army Soldiers Stationed at Fort Huachuca Army Base," McDonald's Corporation, November 11, 2022, https://corporate.mcdonalds.com/corpmcd/our-stories/article/first-mcd-drivethru.html.
2. Martin E. P. Seligman, "Building Resilience," *Harvard Business Review*, April 2011, https://hbr.org/2011/04/building-resilience; Martin E. P. Seligman, *Learned Optimism: How to Change Your Mind and Your Life* (A.A. Knopf, 1991).
3. "Sylvester Stallone: Credits," IMDb, https://www.imdb.com/name/nm0000230/. Britannica, "Sylvester Stallone," updated December 30, 2024, lists *Klute* as among his uncredited appearances: https://www.britannica.com/biography/Sylvester-Stallone.
4. Ben Wyatt, "Chuck Wepner: Honouring the Real-Life 'Rocky' Who Floored Muhammad Ali," BBC Sport, January 26, 2023, https://www.bbc.com/sport/64392108.
5. Sylvester Stallone, interview by Barry Norman, *Film 77*, originally broadcast January 23, 1977, posted January 2, 2022, by BBC Archive, YouTube video, quote begins at 0:58, https://www.youtube.com/watch?v=dFlybZL1mWE.
6. Oliver E. Williams et al., "Quantifying and Predicting Success in Show Business," *Nature Communications* 10 (2019): 2256, https://doi.org/10.1038/s41467-019-10213-0.
7. Mary Gallagher, "Sylvester Stallone Shares Memory of Dog He Sold 'to Buy Food' and Bought Back for £15K," UK Yahoo! Entertainment, March 13, 2017, https://uk.news.yahoo.com/sylvester-stallone-shares-memory-of-dog-he-sold-to-buy-food-and-bought-back-for-15k-101735346.html.
8. Judy Klemesrud, "'Rocky Isn't Based on Me,' Says Stallone, 'but We Both Went the Distance,'" *New York Times*, November 1, 1976, https://archive.nytimes.com/www.nytimes.com/packages/html/movies/bestpictures/rocky-ar.html.
9. "How Sylvester Stallone Went from Homeless Actor to Hollywood Star," WABC, February 22, 2016, https://abc7ny.com/sylvester-stallone-rocky-ii-iii/1204319/.
10. "The Numbers: Rocky (1976)," Nash Information Services, https://www.the-numbers.com/movie/Rocky#tab=summary/; "The Numbers: Top Grossing Movies of 1976," Nash Information Services, https://www.the-numbers.com/market/1976/top-grossing-movies.
11. "This Day in History (January 9): Sylvester Stallone Starts Filming 'Rocky,'" History.com, https://www.history.com/this-day-in-history/stallone-starts-filming-rocky.
12. Sylvester Stallone, interview by Barry Norman, *Film 77*, YouTube video, quote starts at 1:38, https://www.youtube.com/watch?v=dFlybZL1mWE.

13. "Bio: About Sylvester Stallone," accessed January 10, 2025, https://sylvesterstallone.com/bio/; Tom Ward, "The Amazing Story of the Making of 'Rocky,'" *Forbes*, updated December 10, 2021, https://www.forbes.com/sites/tomward/2017/08/29/the-amazing-story-of-the-making-of-rocky/.
14. Valorie Burton, *Where Will You Go from Here? Moving Forward When Life Doesn't Go as Planned* (Colorado Springs, CO: Waterbrook, 2011), 3–6.
15. See Proverbs 18:21, NKJV.
16. John Maxwell, *Failing Forward: Turning Mistakes into Stepping Stones for Success* (Nashville: Thomas Nelson, 2000).
17. Douglas Stone and Sheila Heen, *Thanks for the Feedback: The Science and Art of Receiving Feedback Well* (New York: Viking, 2014), ch. 9.
18. As quoted in Liliana Dell'Osso et al., "Post Traumatic Growth (PTG) in the Frame of Traumatic Experiences," *Clinical Neuropsychiatry* 19, no. 6 (December 2022): 390–393, https://pmc.ncbi.nlm.nih.gov/articles/PMC9807114/.
19. Laura Cappelle, "Why the Top Gymnast in France Is Competing for Algeria," *New York Times*, July 31, 2024, https://www.nytimes.com/2024/07/31/world/olympics/kaylia-nemour-olympics-gymnastics-france-algeria.html; Ashlee Buhler, "French-Born Kaylia Nemour Wins Historic Olympic Gold for Algeria; Suni Lee Claims Bronze," NBC Universal, August 4, 2024, https://www.nbcolympics.com/news/french-born-kaylia-nemour-wins-historic-olympic-gold-algeria-suni-lee-claims-bronze.

RESILIENCE RULE #9: KNOW WHEN TO GRIT, KNOW WHEN TO QUIT

1. Angela L. Duckworth et al., "Cognitive and Noncognitive Predictors of Success," *Proceedings of the National Academy of Sciences* 116, no. 47 (November 4, 2019): 23499–23504, https://doi.org/10.1073/pnas.1910510116.
2. Angela L. Duckworth et al., "Grit: Perseverance and Passion for Long-Term Goals," *Journal of Personality and Social Psychology* 92, no. 6 (June 2007): 1087–1101, https://doi.org/10.1037/0022-3514.92.6.1087.
3. I tell this story and outline these principles at "When to Persevere and When to Let Go," Maxwell Leadership, February 29, 2024, https://www.maxwellleadership.com/blog/persevere-and-let-go/.
4. "The 24 Character Strengths," VIA Institute on Character, accessed January 10, 2025, https://www.viacharacter.org/character-strengths.

RESILIENCE RULE #10: CLOSE YOUR ENERGY GAP

1. Roy F. Baumeister, "Ego Depletion and Self-Control Failure: An Energy Model of the Self's Executive Function," *Self and Identity* 1, no. 2 (2002): 129–136, https://doi.org/10.1080/152988602317319302.
2. Walter Mischel, *The Marshmallow Test: Mastering Self-Control* (Little, Brown and Co, 2014).

3. Michele M. Tugade and Barbara L. Fredrickson, "Resilient Individuals Use Positive Emotions to Bounce Back from Negative Emotional Experiences," *Journal of Personality and Social Psychology* 86, no. 2 (2004): 320–333, https://doi.org/10.1037/0022-3514.86.2.320.
4. Amrisha Vaish et al., "Not All Emotions Are Created Equal: The Negativity Bias in Social-Emotional Development," *Psychological Bulletin* 134, no. 3 (May 2008): 383–403, https://doi.org/10.1037/0033-2909.134.3.383; Barbara Fredrickson, *Positivity: Discover the Upward Spiral That Will Change Your Life* (New York: Harmony, 2009).
5. "Exercise Can Boost Your Memory and Thinking Skills," Harvard Medical School, Harvard Health Publishing, August 26, 2024, https://www.health.harvard.edu/mind-and-mood/exercise-can-boost-your-memory-and-thinking-skills.
6. "Endorphins," Cleveland Clinic, accessed January 10, 2025, https://my.clevelandclinic.org/health/body/23040-endorphins.
7. Sonja Lyubomirsky, *The How of Happiness: A New Approach to Getting the Life You Want* (New York: Penguin, 2008), 20–21.

BONUS RULE: PAY IT FORWARD

1. Jessica Cerretani, "The Contagion of Happiness," *Harvard Medicine*, Summer 2011, https://magazine.hms.harvard.edu/articles/contagion-happiness.
2. Paul Brand and Philip Yancey, *Fearfully and Wonderfully Made* (Grand Rapids, MI: Zondervan, 1980), 82.
3. Stephen Schramm, "Build Your Resilience by Helping Others," Duke Today, December 7, 2020, https://today.duke.edu/2020/12/build-your-resilience-helping-others.
4. Catherine Moore, "What Is Appreciative Inquiry? (Definition, Examples, and Model)," PositivePsychology.com, April 27, 2019, https://positivepsychology.com/appreciative-inquiry/#cooperrider.

ABOUT THE AUTHOR

Valorie Burton is founder of The Coaching and Positive Psychology (CaPP) Institute. Since its launch in 2009, The CaPP Institute has served clients and coaches in over thirty countries through coach training and resilience training. She is also the coaching mentor for more than 55,000 Maxwell Leadership Certified Team members from over 160 countries.

Valorie is a Master Certified Coach, a credential held by fewer than 4 percent of International Coaching Federation members. She helps people build resilience and happiness through her research-based emphasis in the pioneering field of applied positive psychology—the study of what happens when things go right with us.

The author of over a dozen books, including *Successful Women Think Differently*, *It's About Time*, and *Brave Enough to Succeed*. Valorie has been a regular guest on the *Today* show and numerous other media outlets. She has been a speaker for hundreds of organizations, ministries, and government entities, including Google, Apple, NASA, Bank of America, and the US military.

Valorie has a master's degree in applied positive psychology from the University of Pennsylvania, a master's degree in journalism from Florida A&M University, and a bachelor's degree from Florida State University. She and her husband, Jeff, have three children and live on a horse farm near Atlanta. Learn more about her training and resources at valorieburton.com and cappinstitute.com.